Missed
OPS

RIVERHEAD FREE LIBRARY
330 COURT STREET
RIVERHEAD, NY 11901

Missed OPS

WHEN OPPORTUNITY KNOCKS . . .
KNOW WHAT NOT TO DO

Skills and strategies to attract, recognize, and take advantage
of opportunity by observing the masses and doing the opposite.

KEITH NELSON
— AND —
ANTHONY RIENZI

Unrivaled
B O O K S
A Division of Health Communications, Inc.
www.unrivaledbooks.com

Library of Congress Control Number: 2011940945

© 2011 Keith Nelson and Anthony Rienzi

ISBN-13: 978-1-61360-113-6 (paperback)
ISBN-10: 1-61360-113-1 (paperback)
ISBN-13: 978-1-61360-114-3 (e-book)
ISBN-10: 1-61360-114-x (e-book)

All rights reserved. Printed in the United States of America. No part of this publication may be reproduced, stored in a retrieval system or transmitted in any form or by any means, electronic, mechanical, photocopying, recording or otherwise, without the written permission of the authors.

Authors: Keith F. Nelson and Anthony Rienzi
www.Missed-Ops.com
www.OpportunityWillKnock.com
MissedOpsBook@gmail.com
Phone: 864-640-5379
Fax: 864-834-3002

Scripture taken from the New King James Version.Copyright © 1982 by Thomas Nelson, Inc. Used by permission. All rights reserved.[Do not change wording. This is from the publisher and must be this way.]

Unrivaled Books, its logos, and marks are the trademarks of Health Communications, Inc.

Publisher: Unrivaled Books
          3201 SW 15th Street
          Deerfield Beach, FL 33442

Cover design by Justin Rotkowitz
Inside book design and formatting by Dawn Von Strolley Grove

I want to thank all the family, friends, and students
who have inspired and motivated me along the way.
I dedicate this book to one opportunity
I did not miss out on—my wife and best friend Robyn.

Keith Nelson

This book is dedicated to my wife, Karen, and our
three beautiful children, Madison, Isabella, and Antonio,
who I hope seize all the opportunities that come their way.
I also dedicate this book to my nephew Santino, whom God
has given a new heart and the opportunity to experience life.

Anthony Rienzi

A special thank-you to the men and women in the
military and law enforcement who put their lives
on the line every day to protect our freedoms so
we can experience all of life's opportunities.

Contents

Preface

All of us have experienced regret at least once in our lives. We wish we could go back and do things differently. We beat ourselves up with "could haves," "would haves," and "should haves." But if regret did not exist, we might never fully appreciate the value of missed opportunities. They are the pangs and sentiments that alert us to an opportunity that came along and we blew it. And in that way regret can be useful. Just as the pain of touching fire is helpful because it warns us not to repeat the same behavior next time we encounter a flame, regret educates us about the nature of getting burned by missed opportunities.

A missed opportunity may cause us to ask ourselves questions with no apparent answers: "What do I do with myself now?" "I worked so hard to get where I was, how do I start over again?" "Will I get another chance?" "How does this change me as a person?"

Much of the regret or emotional pain of failure, disappointment, and trauma comes from this kind of fundamental disconnect with our own identities. Regret can create what philosophers call an existential crisis—a situation where we question our very existence and the core values that are the foundation of everything we believe about ourselves and the world around us.

When we experience a setback or missed opportunity and find ourselves in a state of regret, we have to deal with that frame of mind or set of emotions in a healthy and proactive way, otherwise it could destroy us emotionally and physically.

Our initial response to regret is to feel bad. But the past is the past, and feeling crummy has never produced anything useful in life. Feeling bad just motivates us to feel even worse. Regret is a powerful emotion that can spiral into more negative feelings. Regret can turn into sadness, anger, rage, depression, sorrow, or fear. The only thing painful regret ensures is that we continue to endure pointless suffering as we give our lives over to negative emotions. Chronic focus on regrettable experiences from the past that are impossible to change or erase only makes the present more difficult to face.

Only when we no longer bear the burden of unnecessary regret and are consciously aware of the ever-changing present moment can we make real, positive changes in our lives.

If only. Those must be the two saddest words in the world.

Mercedes Lackey

Introduction

Have you ever regretted a missed opportunity? How valuable would it be to learn the skills necessary to recognize, create, and, most important, take advantage of opportunities to become successful?

If you are like the authors and millions of other people, you have experienced the regret of missed opportunity. You may have endured the despair of wanting something and failing to reach it. You might have felt the sting of rejection by others. Or you might have simply let a good opportunity slip away because you didn't know how to reel it in and capture it.

Opportunities are the doorways to success. If you are not exactly where you want to be in life or have not achieved the level of success that you dream of, it is because of missed opportunities.

Our lives are a series of opportunities that coincide, reflect, and compound on one another. This often overlooked but simple fact is essential information to succeed at anything you set out to do.

Self-improvement experts, motivational speakers, and life coaches often fail to adequately address the significance of opportunity, but without opportunity there can be no success. The importance of opportunity is immeasurable and cannot be overestimated. The time has come for us to understand exactly how to acquire the skills and strategies to attract, uncover, and create new opportunities.

The next and most critical step to success is how to take full advantage of opportunities.

Imagine yourself a contestant on a game show where you and nine other contestants are given the task of completing a complex maze. The maze has thirteen entryways, but only three lead to the finish line. The rules are simple: any contestant who completes the maze successfully wins a million dollars.

Now imagine you are the last to take your turn, so you can watch every contestant complete the maze from their chosen starting locations before you attempt it. Being last gives you an advantage over all the other contestants. If you went first, the chances of choosing the correct path is only three out of thirteen. It is safe to say the last person to go has the highest percentage chance to succeed. The more people you observe (the more knowledge you gain), the greater your chance of success. Observing the other contestants, even if every one of them chooses the wrong path, gives you an advantage by using their experiences and leveraging it into your own knowledge of how to play a smarter game.

You won't repeat their mistakes by going through the wrong door. Common sense tells you that not following the incorrect paths, as others did, dramatically improves your shot at success. The more failure you observe, the greater your chance of success. In general, using other people's failures can assist you, increasing your chances to succeed by knowing what paths not to take. The same approach can be applied when faced with real-life opportunities.

If opportunities are the doorways to success, then knowing how to succeed at them is the key to those doors. We can accomplish this by first knowing what not to do and working backward from there.

We compiled the processes, skills, and theories outlined in this book by observing, experiencing, and researching the failure of countless missed opportunities, and we offer them to you to give you the ultimate winning advantage.

Just as the contestant who completed the maze learned the successful paths by watching others fail, we too can become successful by learning from the wrong choices and regrets of others' missed opportunities. Our challenge is to hone keen observational skills and practice them until they become instinctual.

This book is an instructional, easy-to-follow guide you can reference when faced with an opportunity to create a more rewarding life by learning the secrets of success from other people's missed opportunities. In other words... observe the masses and do the opposite.

Other self-improvement books outline the paths, skills, and processes of highly successful people and expect you to follow what they did to become just as successful. Following the successful path of one person, or a group of people, is flawed and limiting in principle, because what is successful for others may not work for you. More important, their paths to success will always be different from yours because no two people are alike. The opportunities they started with are not the same as what life hands you. A book written by a person who took a rose-garden path and ended up a fairy-tale multimillionaire may not be as relatable or applicable to your own circumstances. But we can all relate to and learn from the Missed Ops stories of everyday people (included in each chapter), and we can avoid failure and increase the odds of success.

Instead of following the limited guidelines of successful people that may not fit your situation, we implore you to learn how to observe the mistakes the masses make and do the opposite.

We promote the concept that the experience of failure is the best teacher . . . as long as it's someone else's experience. There is unique value in developing the ability to view the outcome of other people's mistakes and gain knowledge as if you personally experienced that mishap.

We also value the significance of blazing your own path and resisting the foolish urge to enthusiastically follow the herd as it goes over a cliff. We implore strategies to avoid living a busy, hectic life that is unproductive and unfulfilling—like a rat trapped on a treadmill.

The information in these pages can have a positive impact on those who have regrets about not taking advantage of past opportunities. Plus it can help those who have not yet made major life decisions to proactively make the best ones the first time around. Learn from the strategies demonstrated in the examples we provide and you will be able to finally break free from chronic cycles of dissatisfaction, failure, and regret.

Missed Ops is about seizing inspirational moments and not letting them slip away into obscurity. Missed Ops demonstrates the regret that "woulda,""shoulda,""coulda" have generated for others. Missed Ops details the pitfalls that prevent us from achieving what we want and points out landmines disguised as buried treasure on the path of life. Missed Ops is your guide or roadmap to successful choices when you encounter opportunities along your unique journey.

HOW TO USE THIS BOOK

❏ Use the experiences of others as the focal point of what not to do when faced with an opportunity. Knowing what paths not to take will drastically increase your chances of success via the process of elimination. The principles described in Missed Ops are founded on this philosophy. Place yourself as the main character in the Missed Op stories, then with the benefit of hindsight and knowing the outcome of the other person's failed opportunity, decide what you would do differently.

❏ Be willing to learn how to improve your life. You might read this book a hundred times, but if you don't desire to learn these tools and apply these techniques, it won't help you in your quest for success.

❏ Have the willpower to persevere. If at first you don't see immediate, positive results from the principles in Missed Op, keep moving in a positive direction.

❏ Use it or lose it. Apply what you have learned; if you don't you will quickly forget it. If you want to master these principles, practice them at every opportunity. Your mind will retain only the knowledge you use, so convert it from book knowledge to personal experience.

❏ Read with a highlighter in hand. When you come across a principle or tool that can help you, highlight it. After reading Missed Ops, keep the book as a resource and revisit it frequently. Highlighting key points will make it easy to rapidly review them when an opportunity presents itself.

❏ Share the book with others—your spouse, coworkers, or friends—so they understand your process and strategy. With their help organize your own think tank and support group. You can observe one another's actions and habits, offering support along the way. Be accountable to yourself and others, and always ask for help from the people around you. We can accomplish greater things with positive encouragement and support.

❏ Examine and review your attempts to capitalize on opportunities as you apply Missed Ops principles to your life. Write down what worked and didn't work, and why. Keep notes on everything so that you can learn from your own experiences as well as from those presented in Missed Ops.

Hindsight is 20/20

– 1 –

Missed Ops gives you the ability to look forward as if you're looking backward. How many times have you looked back on a situation and wished you had made a different choice? How many times have you heard others lament about choices they made, wishing they could change it? Time and time again we hear "hindsight is 20/20" from loved ones, friends, acquaintances, and even strangers.

Every day we meet people who have regretted one or more of the important decisions in their lives. Life becomes hard when you look in the rearview mirror at regret in the choices, decisions, and missed opportunities of the past. People who live life like this reach a point of despair. They begin keeping their heads down while trudging through life, leading to more wrong decisions that seem to compound on one another.

Throughout this book, we will say, "Experience is the best teacher . . . as long as it is someone else's experience," meaning that the ability to view the outcome of other people's mistakes before you make them yourself is priceless. You gain the knowledge and wisdom as if the experience were your own—but without the risk of going through it yourself. How much time, energy, or money can you save by using other people's past experiences to help you evaluate each new opportunity? Imagine how much stress you avoid by making more informed decisions based on someone else's experience.

Time and time again you hear "learn from your mistakes." But why should you have to live through mistakes in order to make educated choices? You do not have to go through that learning process if the knowledge gained from mistakes is available to you. Learning from your mistakes is important, for sure, but learning from the mistakes of others is much more efficient. This applies to school, relationships, business, and almost every other aspect of life.

The process is, however, easier said than done. But in this book we describe simple steps you can take to identify each opportunity and make better decisions. Use the real-life examples and stories about what not to do when faced with an opportunity to help your pursuit toward success. Along the way you will be armed with the information and experience you need to make the best possible choices to accomplish your goals.

Opportunity [n] 1: a favorable juncture of circumstances
                      2: a good chance for advancement or progress

Merriam-Webster

MISSED OP:
Will I Ever Be There Again?

In the summer of 2008 I decided to do two things I had sworn I would never do: go into management, and take an assignment at FBI Headquarters. My family reluctantly agreed to move with me to Washington DC. The kids were off from school, so the timing was right. But adjusting to a different house, new neighbors, and a strange school, with no local family support, were definitely going to be challenges. Knowing all that, it's understandable that I chose to turn down one of the most tantalizing opportunities of my life. Yet I still regret that I did.

At my new assignment, I began talking with an intelligence analyst named Fred. He was former military and one of the sharpest, most thorough and well-rounded people you could ever meet. Fred kept talking about an assignment he seemed reluctant to tackle alone. He was to train a newly formed police department in a small country on the west coast of Africa. It was one of those exotic, highly responsible adventures that people ask you about at cocktail parties! As an FBI special agent, I had dreams of assignments in exotic and foreign places. Man, this was exactly what I'd signed up for!

When I offered to go with him, Fred rushed to show me all of the information we would ever need: pictures of the local area; medical, State Department and military reports; plus historical facts about the region. I knew I was going to be all right traveling with Fred!

The assignment was not without challenges. The government of the third world country was unstable. The economy was struggling. State Department warnings included malaria and other diseases. The FBI doctors administered five shots and gave me pills to take for everything and anything. On top of that, Headquarters told us that because there were no regular flights and it was monsoon season, the trip could be prolonged.

That was when I started having second thoughts about going to Africa while my family was in transition. Soon Fred and I were coming up with excuses not to go. Before we knew it, we canceled the trip.

I felt relief—and regret.

In retrospect, I would give a lot to have that opportunity back. Life passes quickly. The time we have to make decisions is often riddled with emotions that cloud judgment. There are absolutely no guarantees in life or career that you will ever get the same opportunity twice! When faced with a decision or choice, it is wise to step back and consider: Will I ever be here again? Will I ever have this opportunity again?

Will you ever get a second chance? If not, maybe this is the time to seize the moment and do what your deep desires tell you, before it's too late and the opportunity is gone.

WHAT NOT TO DO:

❐ Make a decision without weighing if that opportunity will ever come around again.

ADVICE:

❐ Know your objective(s).

❐ List and analyze the pros and cons, strength and weaknesses, of your available options. Weigh those options carefully.

❐ Discuss the decision with the people who will most be affected; explain your point of view and listen to theirs.

❐ Ask yourself if this opportunity will ever present itself again.

What are the steps to make the right decisions when faced with opportunities? First is the recognition of opportunity, followed by the cognitive or thought process. Cognitive research shows that individuals must possess prior knowledge and the intellectual ability necessary to value that knowledge to identify new options available to them.[1] Last, a prepared and streamlined decision-making process must be put into place. This concept of an individual's mental makeup and process is directly related to his or her ability to identify and take advantage of a presented opportunity.

RECOGNIZING OPPORTUNITIES

Many great opportunities are passed over because people simply don't recognize them. How many opportunities have you recognized only after they have passed you by? Often we see only what is familiar to us, missing incredible opportunities that are right in front of us. It is essential that we not get too attached to one particular idea or way of thinking regarding how success can be achieved. Opportunity is all around us. We just need to step back and open our eyes a little wider to identify it. Whether it involves deepening relationships or finding an entrepreneurial opportunity to become wealthy, we can realize those opportunities that seem to fly past us if we understand how to discover, create, or recognize them.

In 1986, a New York detective named Bob was told about an estate sale in an upper middle-class neighborhood in Suffolk County, New York. The home was priced significantly below the market. Bob told his wife about the property, and she said it was a great time to purchase property. He also discussed it with a friend who owned several rental properties. Bob saw the opportunity staring him in the face and realized its potential, so he bought the house and has been renting it out ever since. He has had a positive cash flow since 1986 and has paid off the mortgage. Bob was presented with an opportunity. He stepped back, recognized the potential, and took advantage of it.

Bob had a fairly straightforward and obvious opportunity. But what if you don't see any opportunities around you?

Opportunities are everywhere. You just have to know where to look and how to discover the less obvious ones.

SURROUND YOURSELF WITH CREATIVE PEOPLE

Creative people can look at a situation and see a better way of handling it. They can approach a problem from a unique point of view or create something out of nothing. But if you do not have that kind of creativity, surround yourself with people who do. Listen to them; they may say or do something that seems routine to them but can unlock a unique opportunity for you.

A friend of mine who worked for a very successful marketing firm in Manhattan invited me to his company's Christmas party. While a woman and I talked about doing laundry, of all things, we discussed how much we hated sorting clothing, especially socks. We agreed that socks that looked alike but were from different pairs were the worst.

Then her creative-thinking coworker chimed in. "You should mark each pair of socks so that you can easily find them and match them together after the wash. You can stitch a color or number onto each sock to make it easy."

What a terribly simple and brilliant idea that was. After a bit of research, we discovered that this idea had been patented five years earlier. But what a valuable lesson I learned. If I surround myself with creative people, a situation, conversation, or event may arise and a valuable opportunity may suddenly and unexpectedly be revealed. You just have to be aware and ready to take advantage of it when it happens.

SEE PROBLEMS AS SOLUTION OPPORTUNITIES

Successful people say there is no such thing as a problem, only opportunities disguised as problems. So when you see a problem, write it down. You may come up with a solution that offers you a gigantic opportunity.

One day in December 1873, Chester Greenwood had to come inside because it was too cold for him to stay outdoors and ice skate. Shivering from the cold, Chester sat at the kitchen table and scribbled on a piece of paper "cold ears means no skating." A few days later he saw his note and thought of a solution to his problem. He found a piece of wire, and with his grandmother's help, padded the ends. Thanks to that simple little invention, he was able to stay outside skating long after his friends had gone inside with freezing ears. At age seventeen, Chester applied for a patent, and for the next sixty years, his factory made earmuffs. And earmuffs made Chester rich.

Carefully define a problem, no matter how insignificant, and then focus on solving it. The simplest solution might just lead you to a spectacular opportunity. Look at a problem from several perspectives. Try changing the question. Ask Who? What? Where? When? Why? And How? to solve it. Change your attitude about problems. Don't see them as roadblocks but as keys that can open new doors that lead to fantastic opportunities. All you have to do is crack the safe with a fresh solution like Chester did.

LISTEN TO OUTRAGEOUS, OUTSIDE-THE-BOX IDEAS

Don't discard an idea just because it sounds too far-out or strange. Give it some time to sink in. Then look at it again. Even if the idea or plan seems impossible or unbelievable, an opportunity may be hiding somewhere in there. Possibly it applies to another problem, or there is a different angle you haven't considered.

Or you might hear an idea that sounds so improbable that people scoff and laugh when they hear it. That might be the rare idea that is just crazy enough to work. They laughed at Christopher Columbus and the Wright

Brothers. When Ben Franklin flew a kite with metal attached to it during an electrical storm, everyone knew he was nuts.

Then there was Gary Dahl. In April, 1975, he was in a bar listening to his friends complain about their pets. This gave him the idea for the perfect pet: a rock. A rock would not need to be fed, walked, bathed, or groomed, and it would never die, become sick, or be disobedient. He said they were the perfect pets, and joked about it with his friends. But the idea haunted him until he seriously considered it. One day Gary decided to go for it. He drafted an instruction manual for a "pet rock." It was full of puns, gags, and plays on words that referred to the rock as an actual pet. The first Pet Rocks were nothing more than ordinary gray stones bought at a builder's supply store. But they were marketed like live pets, in custom cardboard pet containers complete with straw and breathing holes. The Pet Rock fad lasted only about six months, ending after a short burst in sales during the 1975 Christmas season. But during their short run, Pet Rocks made Dahl a millionaire, and his quirky idea is still considered one of the greatest entrepreneurial schemes of all time.

GROUP BRAINSTORMING

Brainstorming is a popular tool that helps generate creative solutions to problems but also can be used to discover new opportunities. Brainstorm in a relaxed and informal environment. Invite one or more people who have positive attitudes and the desire and determination to succeed. Inviting people from different fields of work will give the group diverse points of view and varied ways of initiating new ideas. Appoint one person to record the ideas that come out of the session. You might consider using an icebreaker activity to get everyone more comfortable, and then start talking about problem solving.

Gradually move into lateral thinking, which is reasoning that is not immediately obvious or directly connected to the problem at hand, but is about less tangible creative ideas. It is fine if you drift far away from your original topic, because it might lead to something no one has thought of yet.

Ideas may even seem a bit crazy, but remember not to dismiss an idea because it is too far-fetched. Some of those wild and crazy ideas can be crafted into original, creative, practical solutions to a problem, and others may spark more ideas. The aim of this group brainstorming approach is to get people thinking outside their comfort zones. That often leads to outside-the-box ideas and the creation of new opportunities.

PRIOR KNOWLEDGE

Individuals must possess prior knowledge to identify and act on new events presented to them. This is where Missed Ops becomes an invaluable tool for future decisions. Gain that necessary knowledge from the stories of Missed Ops (opportunities) sprinkled throughout the book. Use those people's experiences and wrong decisions to help you make the right choices. We are bombarded with many resources telling us what we should do, but none that tells us what happens if we chose the wrong options or do nothing at all.

No two opportunities are identical, and yours may seem very different from the many stories of real people in this book. But you can adapt them to your situation, because the principles behind them are universal. Make use of them by treating them as your own prior knowledge. These stories can save you a lot of time, stress, money, and energy. Making all of those wrong decisions for yourself would take a lifetime of experience. But all you have to do is read about them and then adopt these valuable experiences as your own.

As an example, franchising is a popular business model that leverages prior knowledge and the experience of others into entrepreneurial success. Franchising is the practice of outlining what works well for a business and then duplicating it for another company without having to repeat their mistakes. A franchise is usually created by taking a business with a good record of profitability and creating easy-to-follow guidelines to replicate its success. In other words, you use another business owner's experience as prior knowledge to streamline your own decision-making process and reduce the chance of failure.

The same principle applies to Missed Ops. The tools and resources in this book basically franchise the prior knowledge and experiences of other people, allowing you to use that information to create your own success in life. But you have the unique advantage of doing it without having to pay the tuition of repeated failure while learning from the school of hard knocks.

INTELLECTUAL ABILITY

You don't have to put any effort into acquiring intellectual ability because either you have it or you don't. But if you have the foresight to recognize Missed Ops as an important resource, it is apparent that you have ample intellectual ability. Your intelligence is the machine that will process the stories and experiences you read about in Missed Ops and then adapt them to your particular situations as useful, helpful, valuable information.

DECISION-MAKING PROCESS

Taking advantage of any opportunity means making decisions. The right decisions will lead to success and the wrong decisions will lead to regret. Making a decision is a process. Using that process to make good decisions on a regular basis takes practice over time. But it is an acquired skill that can be learned by anyone.

Schools teach many important subjects that prepare us for life and enable us to become contributing members of society. Subjects like math, science, economics, health, and, of course, wood shop all have value. But far too little instruction is given to decision making and goal setting. Isn't being happy in life and satisfied with the choices we make immensely important? So it is up to us to apply the repetition and practice methods we used to learn math or English to learn how to efficiently make decisions.

One of the most influential books I have ever read is Dale Carnegie's How to Win Friends and Influence People. The principles discussed in that book transcend time. They are not bound by culture or education. What an awesome book! But by the same token, what a basic book! It is one of the most popular self-development books ever written because we constantly need to be reminded of the simpler things that we already know through formal or informal education and experience.

Decision making is one factor that influences the direction of your whole life more than any other thing. It is likely to have a greater effect than the people skills imparted by Dale Carnegie, or even your level of formal education. The most important time to make the right decision is as soon as an opportunity reveals itself to you. It is imperative to spot opportunities and make choices that are ideal for you and your future.

When making a decision:

❒ Know your objectives and place them in order of importance or priority. Anticipate what could be or what is probable and possible.

❒ List and analyze the pros and cons, or strengths and weaknesses, of your available options. Weigh those options carefully, research and seek expert advice on each and every one of them.

❒ Ask yourself if this opportunity will ever present itself to you again. Some opportunities are a one-time-only offer and you have to grab them before they slip through your fingers.

❒ Accept the positive and negative input of others. But make sure you know where their advice is coming from or how they derived it; then evaluate that advice against your objectives.

❒ Make a tentative decision and then further evaluate it to look for additional possible consequences.

❒ Take decisive action and finalize your decision. Create an action plan if necessary.

❒ Adapt to changing situations and adjust your original decision accordingly.

❒ Review your decision after some time has passed. Write down what went right and if anything went wrong. The physical act of writing down this information will ingrain it further into your mind and teach you, through your own experience, what the right course of action was. Use this important information to help you make your next decision.

The more practice you have at the decision-making process, the better you will become at developing a more efficient procedure. Making decisions by using this procedure will become easier over time until the skill becomes second nature. Some opportunities are time sensitive, though, and demand a quick decision. So it is imperative that you become proficient at the decision-making process as soon as possible. If you are already practicing these methods and preparing yourself to seize your opportunity, you are one step closer to making your dreams a reality.

Remember, learning how to recognize opportunities and then applying a sound decision-making process (coupled with using other people's experiences) will put you in a better position to exploit an opportunity when one presents itself.

Success always comes when preparation meets opportunity.

Henry Hartman

MISSED OP:
Bungalow Blunder

My brothers and I spent several years building a contracting business, but we eventually decided it was time for a career change. We sold it to my friend's brother, Brad, who slowly continued to build the company. After a few years, Brad had built a loyal client base—a practice that paid off. One of his more important clients was obviously impressed by his dedication and potential, and she relied on him to maintain her twenty rental properties. She offered to sell him one of the properties—a cozy bungalow on a beautiful canal in an affluent Long Island, New York neighborhood—for $70,000, which, even in those days, was a great bargain. To sweeten the deal, she even promised to hold the mortgage and didn't require any cash up front.

Brad was uncertain; he still felt unsure in the business and didn't have a steady cash flow. Without spending much time considering the consequences, he concluded that the immediate risks seemed to outweigh the benefits. Today, that property is worth over $700,000; the plot of land with the tiny bungalow continues to increase.

It is unsurprising that now, with the infallible glasses of hindsight to peer through, Brad feels that he made a terrible error in choosing to pass up an incredible investment opportunity. When he looked at the situation, all he saw were potential pitfalls, which overshadowed the immense profit he could have made. It is irrelevant whether the thoughts of future failure that paralyzed him were born of fear or distraction. What matters is he lost the fortune because he was unable to distance himself enough—or find someone else to do it for him—to make a logical decision unhindered by a disproportionate amount of fear. Had he stepped back and examined possible influential factors— the trend of property value growth or population growth in the area, the proximity of the area to large metropolises, and any changes in property values projected by experts—it is likely that he would have made a different choice. Alternatively, if he felt too close to the situation—as many of us often find ourselves—he could have sought advice from an experienced real-estate investor or partnered with a creative financial adviser. Either way, a distanced opinion might have averted one of the greatest financial mistakes of Brad's life.

WHAT NOT TO DO:

❏ Make a hasty decision that causes failure to see an opportunity.

ADVICE:

❏ Step back and look at the larger picture.
❏ Ask a successful real-estate investor's advice.

PARENTS: What Do They Really Know?

−2−

What is involved in rearing children? Most people would say providing food, shelter, clothing, health care, education, and other basic necessities of life. But what do parents really know about guiding their offspring to become successful adults?

Sometimes parenthood is planned, while other times it is not. In either case moms and dads are constantly tested on their abilities to parent. Caring for children takes a lot of time and energy. Child rearing is even harder when the parents have problems of their own, such as worries about their jobs, bills, or relationships. With an eye on keeping their children safe, parents teach their offspring to act certain ways or to avoid certain situations. But even good parents make mistakes; everyone makes mistakes. It is human nature not to be perfect. So children grow up with habits, fears, and doubts, which can work against them when aiming for toward their goals.

If your parents did the best job they could and you aren't where you want to be in life, then maybe it is time to start unlearning some of the things that you were conditioned for while growing up. One important realization is that parents can teach only what they have learned; their life experiences and their past guidance dictate how they raise their offspring. What is important to learn here is that one generation draws from the previous generation and passes those experiences on to the next generation.

MISSED OP:
Helpful Financial Advice:
Take It with a Grain of Salt

I know a hard-working woman in her early forties who was still in high school when she read in a magazine about retirement accounts and how they work. The thought of putting away a small percentage of income every week or every month and then watching it grow and compound in value over time—automatically and without any extra effort or work—fascinated the teenager. She thought it was the best idea she had ever heard. The concept of making money work for her rather than just working hard for money was brilliant. She wanted to put the idea into practice without delay.

Most of her teenage friends preferred to spend money and not worry about saving it for anything, especially a far-off retirement plan. A trip to the mall was their idea of an intelligent way to manage money, because, after all, they were young and had plenty of time to worry about budgeting and saving when they got older and had more grown-up responsibilities.

Her parents advised the adolescent to build up her credit rating if she wanted to prepare for the future. "Instead of setting up a retirement saving account, you should get your own credit card." They helped set her up with her own plastic and soon she was racking up unnecessary debt by buying CDs, shoes, and pizza.

Looking back she is amazed at how bad that advice turned out to be. "I could be retired by now if I had started saving thirty years ago," she says. "But instead I got caught up on the treadmill of being a typical consumer and considering credit card debt as a fact of adult life."

Of course we cannot expect teenagers to go to professional financial planners. But parents can. They should at least read books or take advantage of other available resources that offer practical, appropriate tips on how to teach teens about money. The difference that kind of informed help and expert advice makes could be life changing, and it may very well determine whether those children grow up saddled with debt or liberated by the experience of being independently wealthy.

WHAT NOT TO DO:
❐ Take advice without being completely informed.

ADVICE:
❐ Research your idea and lay out a plan.
❐ Seek advice from several sources.

We should listen carefully to the advice of good parents and others who are concerned for our well-being, because the words of wisdom they impart to us may be golden. But no matter how much they love us, they may not be the most financially savvy people on the planet. So it is also strongly recommended that before actually following the financial advice of others—or doling it out to our kids—we should get a second opinion from someone with proven expertise in such matters.

THE APPLE DOESN'T FALL FAR FROM THE TREE

The famous song "Cats in the Cradle" by Harry Chapin portrays the reality that a child turns out like his or her parents. It's evident from the song and statistical research[2] that from a young age, children learn parenting skills and viewpoints from their moms and dads. Therefore, the saying "The apple doesn't fall far from the tree" means children's actions and behaviors are like those of their parents. But what if your parents' tree isn't your favorite type of tree? What if you want to be different from your parents? We're not suggesting that you don't love them or that they don't love you; rather, if you want to be different, it's okay. But how do you plan to be different? Consciously or subconsciously, children copy their parents' traits. Statistics show that kids of an alcoholic parent are four times more likely to become alcoholics themselves, and children who were abused have a 35 percent greater chance to abuse their children.[3] If those statistics are from proven data, then simple logic would state the same is true for other categories that aren't studied, such as finance, business, and personal relationships. Children of successful people imitate their parents' irrepressible optimism and confidence, and embrace a life of chasing their dreams. I have interviewed many self-made millionaires and one surprising bit of information I learned is that most of these parents are against giving their children any type of inheritance or extravagant allowance. There are the over-popularized cases like the Hiltons and Rockefellers. Then there are parents like Warren Buffett, who is ranked by Forbes magazine as the second-richest billionaire. Buffett is so insistent that his children make their own way that when his daughter, Susie, asked for a home-improvement loan, he told her to go to the bank. Most successful, self-made millionaires want to pass down to their children the same drive and determination that made them successful.

If you're surrounded by hard-working, middle-class folks, chances are you will turn out to be a hard-working, middle-class adult as well. Of course, some people break the mold and jump from the lower or middle class and become ultra-successful. But many who do this can throw a baseball 95 miles per hour, or run a 40-yard dash in 4.5 seconds. Just look at how the population is spread between the classes and how the classes change from year to year and decade to decade. Studies show that in America, 42 percent of financial wealth is controlled by the top 1 percent of the population.[4] If we break the data down further, we find that 93 percent of all financial wealth is controlled by the top 10 percent of the country. The old saying "The rich get richer and the poor get poorer" illustrates well what happens if we continue to do what we know. If you fit into the majority of the population, then you are left dreaming and contemplating and sometimes planning what to do to get everything you want in life. Wouldn't it be great if you could make those dreams a reality? You can! Make those dreams a reality by learning from other people's experiences and analyzing the advice you receive.

EDUCATION AND SECURITY

In lower through upper middle-class neighborhoods, getting a good education and a good job are preached over and over to kids. In a poor economy, having a good job and good education might not be enough, or you might simply want more than that. Even in a good economy, having a good education and a good job may allow you just to keep up with the never ending increases in daily expenses. Either way, settling for something will almost always lead to disappointment, resentment, or unhappiness.

Most parents want the very best for their children, so they encourage and advise them on what they think is the right path for their children. But is it enough to raise them to be safe by getting a good job and becoming self-sufficient? Are you satisfied with self-sufficient and safe? What child grows up dreaming he or she wants to become self-sufficient?

Other parents fill the caregiver role but do not give clear, expressed direction. In a family with more than one child, parents often don't individualize their children's plans for the future. Instead of evaluating each child's skills, talents, and desires, parents often take a cookie-cutter approach, where one path is acceptable for all siblings. When I was growing up, that general notion was go to college, get a stable job, get married, have kids, and start the process over again. It is now up to you to inject the phrase and to become as successful as I can imagine. Going to college was a staple in middle-class Long Island, New York. It was implied that you were supposed to go, and there was no discussion otherwise. A number of highly successful people didn't agree or follow that plan. Walt Disney dropped out of school at age sixteen, Henry Ford stopped going to school and left home to become a machinist at the age of seventeen, and Milton Hershey had only a fourth-grade education. You could argue that those were different times and opportunities were bountiful. But that reasoning didn't stop Michael Dell (CEO of Dell Computers) from dropping out of university at nineteen; Steve Jobs (founder of Apple) left college after one semester; Mary Kay Ash (founder of a cosmetics empire) didn't attend college at all; and Woody Allen (famous director) flunked out because of poor grades. Take note: we are not telling you that college is unimportant, but if you have a passion in life, following that desire and achieving your goals might not take you down the same road it takes others. Think of your dreams, create your goals, weigh all options, seek guidance, and analyze all advice before making a life-altering decision.

IF YOU WANT WHAT YOUR PARENTS HAVE, DO WHAT THEY DID

While growing up I didn't know many parents who encouraged their kids to shoot for something out of the ordinary. It wasn't their fault; working-class families breed working-class children. They knew it was a difficult enough world without taking life-changing risks, and they could educate their children only from their own life experiences. What if your parents asked what your dreams are and how you planned to go about achieving them? What if your parents encouraged you to plan or to take risks or to think outside of the box? If you didn't have parents who did this for you, it is never too late or too early to start a new game plan for the future.

One of the most successful people in American history is a man who chose his own path despite the advice from others. Bill Gates dropped out of Harvard, an elite Ivy League school, in his junior year to start what was to become the largest computer software company in the world: Microsoft Corporation.

Supporting a child in a decision and guiding him or her through it are two totally different things. Good parents will support their children's decisions, but prepared parents will guide them to make the best possible choices for any given situation. Prepared parents will show their children how to research information on the topic, how to weigh the positives and negatives, and how to seek expert advice outside their comfortable advice pool. If someone had sat you down, showed you how to outline your goals, and helped you work backward from there, your chances for success would be multiple times greater than the average person. What if your parents encouraged you to take certain calculated risks, to think outside the box? Could you have ended up in the same spot? Would you have ended up in a worse position? Possibly, but you could have become an ultra-successful, confident overachiever who dreams big and makes their dreams happen. If you want what your parents have, then do what they did; if you want something different or greater, then start researching and calculating your own path.

Take calculated risks. That is quite different from being rash.

George S. Patton

MISSED OP:
Small Business Owner

Kevin, a twenty-one-year-old college student, had a passion for exploring new opportunities to make money. An avid entrepreneur at heart, Kevin had searched endlessly for the chance to make some extra cash. Many people told him he was wasting his time looking for what they called a quick, money-making fix. In his quest to conquer such dreams, he had sought the help of friends, most of whom did not support his dream. Yet he had this passion for making money on his own. His family had an opinion, which they repeated. Clearly, they didn't support him.

However, the seeds to make his dream come true had taken root. Kevin was determined to form a business of his own. This idea started modestly, but quickly grew into a great idea—one that would serve him well financially for the rest of his life.

But everyone, including Mom, Dad, and Grandpa, had the right idea, or so they thought: Kevin should go to college and become civil servant. It would serve him well through life. Even Aunt Ruby thought he should be a teacher or a police officer—anything that required an education.

But Kevin's plans were somewhat different. His plan was to take matters into his own hands. Night after night, he worked on his laptop, scouring the Internet for his dream job, often to no avail. Just when he was about to give up, something wonderful happened. He was browsing a website for young professionals when he stumbled upon a great resource for an aspiring entrepreneur like himself. Few people knew about it: a state-owned concession, located on state park property.

After eagerly filling out all the necessary paperwork and pitching a proposal to the state board of directors, Kevin was awarded a four-year contract to run a seasonal state concession. The first year was painful. Kevin would begin work at 5 am and wrap up the day at 10 or 11 at night. All job responsibilities fell solely on him—the young, inexperienced businessman. Though he had to work long hours, he managed to make it work. By this time, the money had started rolling in.

After the season ended, Kevin was exhausted, but satisfied that he had done a good job and made a nice salary. He was making much more than anyone else his age. And though he should have been happy, he couldn't have felt more miserable. The second season was a little easier, but the hours hadn't changed. They were still long and left him feeling fatigued. Toward the end of the second season, Kevin's family started asking when he was going to go back to school and finish his bachelor's degree. They wanted him to get a stable job with proper health and dental insurance.

His family was made up mostly of blue- and white-collar civil servants. Most were college graduates who got modest-paying jobs with the city and state. They worked as teachers, police officers and firemen. But they viewed Kevin's business as a temporary job that lacked stability.

Every time Kevin visited his family, they tried to talk him into giving up his business and getting a stable job after he graduated college. His family tried to persuade him to make what they considered the safer decision, even though he was banking more money than anyone who was giving him advice.

All the negatives of the business world glared at him each day he went to work. Eventually all the advice Kevin had gotten on life and his career choice began to take its toll.

He hired someone to run the business the following season while he went back to school. His college was 100 miles away from his business. This situation did not work out well. Everyone he hired was a walking disaster and hurt more than they helped. Before long, he was getting phone calls from state supervisors, asking why he wasn't around to handle problems. During the final year of the contract, he decided not to renew. He was convinced that what he was doing was temporary. Going back to school and getting a stable job was the smart option. In the eyes of his family, it was the only option.

Looking back on that decision, Kevin feels remorse, and he resents his family for leading him away from his dreams. "Why in the world would I give up a six-figure salary for stability? If I had gotten better advice, I could have kept the business and invested my huge salary. I could have been retired in ten years instead of thirty years working at my current civil service position."

Had he kept his job, Kevin would have been able to retire sooner and enjoy financial independence at a younger age. "Doing that would be impossible in my current, civil service position," Kevin thought ruefully.

WHAT NOT TO DO:

❒ Follow business advice from people who are where you don't want to be.

ADVICE:

❒ Analyze the source of advice. When parents and family give advice, they are typically regurgitating what they have learned.

ADVICE POOL

Parents, teachers, coaches, friends, and other family members make up our advice pool, which is somewhat limited by our social standing and the neighborhoods we grew up in. An important step in achieving what you want is to realize that when you search for information regarding an important decision, listen to the information from your advice pool, but also look outside of it for a different perspective. Unless your advice pool has had an identical experience in the same time period, you might wonder if they are equipped to give the best advice on a matter. Advice is not just limited to financial or career choices; it could include relationships or personal issues as well. Nonetheless, the same principles apply; people can give advice based only on what they have experienced. For example, you want advice about breaking up with a girlfriend or boyfriend to pursue a relationship with someone else. If someone from your advice pool has had only one serious relationship and he married his girlfriend, is he equipped to give a nonbiased opinion? His advice all depends on the outcome of his decision about his relationship. If he has a happy, healthy relationship with his wife, his advice might sway in one direction; if he's had a miserable life thus far, he might advise you in a different direction. If you understand where people are coming from, you can better evaluate their advice.

During childhood, we don't have much input or control over whom we interact with or learn from. Growing up we get all sorts of counsel from the advice pool. It becomes incumbent upon us to evaluate all that information and compute a response for every situation we face. At a young age, because we need protection, information, and training for the future, we are trained and conditioned to listen to our advice pool without analyzing where that guidance is coming from. At what age does our advice pool start to hinder rather than help us? I can remember back to my toddler days playing in the sandbox with other children. If I saw a shiny toy that another kid had, I would waddle over and take it; I wanted something I did not possess, and most children are the same way. My mother would do the responsible thing and reprimand me. "You can't just take something because you want it." How many times are children told that they can't have this, or they shouldn't ask for that? What type of conditioning does this translate into when we are older? We are conditioned that we can't have what we want just because we want it, which defeats us, convincing us that if something seems too far out of reach, then we can't get it—like a house in Beverly Hills, the perfect spouse, six-pack abs, or financial freedom to do what we want when we want.

Another instance of solid advice while growing up but hindering us as we get older is risk taking, which is part of our human nature. We have been warned and conditioned our entire lives about risks. The concept of risk solely exists because we don't know how certain events will turn out. Out of caution for our safety, adults tell children not to take risks: look both ways before crossing the street, because if you don't you could get hit by a car; don't run with scissors, you might stab yourself; tie your shoelaces because you will trip and fall. All of those repeated tales of caution can be interpreted and overstressed in other adult risk-taking situations. Our society reinforces and plays on the negatives and fears of risks, just as we learned as children. We are conditioned and reinforced to play it safe, making it the most common reason people don't make the best of a presented opportunity. If you take an investment risk, you can lose money; if you try skydiving, you can lose your life; if you tell your boss your way is better than his, you could lose your job; and if you ask that woman out, you could lose your pride.

Because of the fear and negativity our conditioning has taught us, we slow down when a perceived risk approaches. Slowing down and approaching overcautiously only hurts ourselves in the pursuit of our goals. We must retrain the way we look at risks; we have to look at each risk as an opportunity to achieve our goals and dreams, not as an opportunity to get hurt.

Start by taking small risks, something to put you out of your comfort zone. Try talking to someone new at work, or speaking up at the next meeting or gathering you attend. You will eventually realize there is nothing to fear but the fear itself. Use smaller risks as practice to work your way up. Progress slowly to larger risks. Start a new hobby like rock climbing or salsa dancing. You will recondition yourself to accept risk taking as a tool to achieve success and happiness. When that next opportunity comes along, you will be ready to take action toward it.

These are only a couple instances where advice at a young age is helpful and necessary but needs to change as we get older. Most parents do not adapt that philosophy for us. It is up to us now to unlearn some of that advice that was beneficial as a child but hinders our success today.

Don't blame your parents because you never accomplished your dreams or goals. It is not your parents' fault; they were conditioned in an ongoing cycle to follow what their parents taught them. Each generation is different; each generation is presented with different opportunities. Using the same directional guidelines that your parents used with you and their parents used with them might not be the best option for success at this time. Now is the time to break the cycle. Step back and look at your situation; evaluate your talents, skills, and desires to prepare a game plan for the future.

Chances are if you are reading this you want more . . . more money, more power, more happiness, or just more of everything. You can and will get it if believe in yourself and learn from other people's mistakes. Don't take blind risks; take calculated risks to improve your chances of success.

I owe my success to having listened respectfully to the very best advice, and then going away and doing the exact opposite.

G. K. Chesterton

American
Idol-ized

— 3 —

Summer faded into fall, and with the change of seasons and the kids returning to school came a new daily grind and weekly routine. Every week had a Tuesday and every Tuesday had a Tuesday night. Why was that night any different than any other? Because, of course, it was American Idol night. My wife and kids couldn't wait to sit on the couch and watch the program, along with millions of other Americans, as thousands of individuals—males, females, teens, adults, cops, waitresses, and even semi-professional singers—sang for their dreams. They had put their lives on hold, traveled across the country, and even faced fear and humiliation. But for what? All for one common goal! To be the next American Idol!

Why would someone want to be the next American Idol? Money? Fame? Travel? I'm not sure. But I am sure that every one of the contestants has compelling reasons, passions, and motivations.

So how about my wife and kids? What did they get out of watching the top twenty-four contestants compete for the coveted title? Well, for one thing, they each had their favorites. One season it was a blonde gospel-country singer; the next year a tattooed waitress. Then came a matronly British woman and a seventeen-year-old heartthrob. But beyond rooting for their annual favorites, what did they gain? Did the show send them a check for watching? Did the winner send them free concert tickets? Did they make contacts that would help them get where they want to go in life? No, no, and no. Millions of Americans spent hours watching the contestants shoot for their goals and dreams. Year after year and season after season, my family couldn't wait for "their" show to come on again, just so they could sit on the couch and watch someone else achieve their goals and dreams.

How about you? What are your dreams? What goals have you set for yourself? What do you want to do with your life?

Maybe you, like me, want to wake up every morning to sip the local coffee while sitting on a balcony and enjoying the view of palm trees. Perhaps you want to be an entrepreneur who earns an income that allows you to buy whatever you want while ignoring price tags because money is no object. Maybe you have friends or family members who could use financial help or you have a desire to be a philanthropist and support charity. Some people want to travel the world and live in fine hotels, eating room service meals prepared by famous chefs.

But whatever your dreams or goals happen to be, I'd bet the farm on one thing. You will not achieve it while sitting on the sofa watching the tube. Whether it's American Idol, Court TV, Jersey Shore, or your favorite sports teams, it is irrelevant. The point is that spending your precious time as a couch potato is not going to advance you toward the realization of your lifelong dreams.

Now don't take this the wrong way. Happiness in this life is achieved through balance, and everyone needs to relax and unwind. Sometimes that involves hanging out on the sofa doing nothing, and that's okay. But you also need to plan and persistently work toward your goals, whether they are related to career, education, relationships, or any other aspect of your life. Then others will be watching you as you achieve your goals and dreams.

Don't get "American Idolized." Don't squander your time watching others achieve what they want out of life. Visualize your own goals. Make a plan to achieve them. Set it in motion. Take action and start working toward the realization of your dreams before life passes you by and all you have left to show for it is couch time in front of the TV.

STOP THE INACTION

Inaction results in the absence of a desire to expend effort, a lack of clear direction, confused goals, or an apathetic attitude. Stop being lazy! Make a conscious decision to change your life in a proactive way. Anyone can come home from work or school and sit down and watch television. This kind of behavior is taking the path of least resistance, which leads to an uneventful and mundane existence. But if you follow the success strategies and tools derived from dissecting a missed opportunity, it is possible to achieve everything you want in life.

The tools are not going to be easy to master, however, because it isn't easy to change old habits and deeply ingrained behaviors. Nobody finds it easy to suddenly do productive work if they don't feel like it and aren't accustomed to it. Accepting failure and rejection isn't easy, and neither is making sacrifices, staying motivated, or remaining focused. Stepping out of your comfort zone is, well, uncomfortable. What we are telling you will take time, practice, and willpower.

But realize that the path of life most people are on right now is also not easy. It's no fun to look at the price tag and realize you cannot afford the item. Nobody enjoys being overweight and unable to break the cycle of bad habits and start a program of eating healthier and exercising. Nobody likes being dissatisfied with his financial situation, her relationship, or his job. It is never easy to sit on the sidelines while others compete. While they are winning, you're stuck in the same old rut. In other words, if you aren't satisfied with your life right now, then your current experience is more difficult to endure than the effort to change and improve your life.

To stop being inactive, you must first visualize what you want in life. Then set goals and list the things you have to do to achieve them. If some things seem overwhelming, break them down into smaller and more easily attainable goals to avoid becoming discouraged. Remember, "Yard by yard is hard; inch by inch it's a cinch."

Start by doing one thing. Take one rewarding baby step, and then all you have to do is keep putting one foot ahead of the other. Through gradual daily progress a little acorn becomes a mighty tree. Build a routine and be persistent. Persistence builds momentum, and that puts the wind at your back, which turns into progress. Then the progress becomes even faster and easier.

Force yourself to take action, especially when you don't feel like it, because that builds grit and determination. Continue moving forward and always reward yourself for your accomplishments. This helps you to stay motivated. Last but not least, don't be upset when you fail. Success is just around the bend, and setbacks are part of the process and the journey.

Remind yourself that your success and progress are much greater than the minor setbacks and failures, so you are still on an upward and forward trajectory. If you're taking ten steps forward for every one or two you slip back, you're winning at least 80 percent of the time; anyone can get rich earning an 80 percent return on his investment.

If you have ever gotten into an exercise routine, you likely understand the satisfaction of being persistent. Your body becomes responsive to the endorphins released during exercise, and mental imagery helps you to associate your routine with doing something positive. Then when you exercise, positive feelings automatically occur, which means you start to look forward to exercising. The same will happen if you establish routines pursuant to your goals. The mind connects the positive habits you create to positive feelings, an improved outlook, and a sense of self-worth. But what happens when those routines stop? The upbeat feelings slip from enthused and energized to lackadaisical and regretful. So it is essential to take action and get into a positive routine that will naturally build upon itself.

Once you start, your mind will offer you plenty of support and encouragement. The task will not only become easier, but you'll look forward to and enjoy the effort you expend. It can lift you out of a slump or depression and give you a whole new lease on life; the journey becomes as satisfying and rewarding as the destination.

By reading this book you have taken the first step to reaching your goals. Creating a solid game plan to achieve your goals and putting that plan into action will make it easier to notice opportunities when they come your way, create new ones, and prepare yourself to act on them. Maybe someone already taught you some of this information so it seems fundamental, but it is essential to learn it well and some of it deserves repeating. Being reminded to use these tools may, in fact, be all the prompting you need to propel you to where you want to be.

VISUALIZE

Visualization is a mental technique that uses your imagination to make your dreams come true. Visualization uses the power of the mind and harnesses the power behind every success. First, create a "big picture" of what you want to do with your life and clearly visualize your goals and dreams in your mind's eye. Visualization can attract the things we desire: health, money, possessions, work, people, and love.

Visualization is powerful and can bring you what you desire, but the opposite is also true. If you picture what you don't want, you will draw it toward you, as well. Most people dwell on negative events, and they tend to think how unlucky they are, but those thoughts and feelings create or manifest more negative events in their lives. Negativity is a self-fulfilling prophecy, but positivity can also be self-fulfilling, so choose it instead and visualize success, not failure.

For now just picture yourself with all the things you desire. See those in your mind and pay attention to all the details. Now, feel the emotion that's associated with those thoughts. See yourself having whatever it is you want in the moment. After you have seen and felt your dreams, it is now time to think of one or more goals you can set to get you there.

FAKE IT UNTIL YOU MAKE IT

Act as if you are already in the place you want to be. While you are pursuing your goals, take on the attitudes, beliefs, and habits of already having achieved them. Acting this way can lead to discovering or creating opportunities that previously didn't exist.

Goals determine what you're going to be.

Julius Erving

SETTING GOALS

In the book What They Don't Teach You in the Harvard Business School, author Mark McCormack describes a study that was conducted on students in the 1979 Harvard MBA program. Students were asked about their goals. Three percent of the graduates had written goals and plans; 13 percent had unwritten goals; and 84 percent had no specific goals at all. Ten years later they were interviewed again, and 13 percent of those who had unwritten goals were earning approximately twice as much as the 84 percent who had no goals at all. Meanwhile, the 3 percent who had clearly written and articulated goals and plans were earning, on average, ten times as much as the other 97 percent combined.[5]

Goal setting is essential. The process helps you choose where you want to go in life. It is a powerful way to get you thinking about and visualizing your ideal future while motivating you to turn your vision into a reality. By identifying exactly what you want to accomplish, you know where you have to focus your efforts. By setting distinct goals you can spot distractions that would otherwise derail you from your objectives. Goal setting helps organize your time and gives you a way to see and benchmark your forward progress toward objectives that might otherwise seem unattainable. In addition, setting and achieving goals is highly motivating and keeps you moving in the right direction. Goal setting provides short- and long-term vision and is utilized by top-tier athletes, world-class entrepreneurs, billion-dollar business owners, and a host of other highly successful and driven people.

Set your goals high, and don't stop till you get there.

Bo Jackson

If you do not yet know what goals you should set, brainstorm some of the following categories and questions to give you general ideas of importance and priority.

CAREER:

❒ What are your interests or hobbies?

❒ Can those be turned into an occupation?

❒ If you already have a satisfying job or career, what level do you ultimately want to reach?

FAMILY:

❒ Do you want to be a parent?

❒ If you are already a parent, do you want to enhance that role and relationship with your children?

❒ Do you want to be closer to a sibling or other relative?

EDUCATION:

❒ Where do you want to go to school, and what grades do you want to achieve?

❒ Do you want an Associate, Bachelor, Master, or Doctorate degree?

❒ What type of education and training will you need to achieve your goals?

SKILLS:

❒ Do you want to learn a craft, technical skill, computer program, new language? How to dance, play music, or be a gourmet chef?

❒ What type of practical skills will you need to achieve your goals?

FINANCIAL:

❒ How much net worth do you want, and within what time frame do you want to reach that target?

❒ Do you want to own property, stock, an antique car, a yacht, or your own airplane?

PERSONAL:

❒ Are there any bad habits you would like to break?

❒ Would you like to be more positive in your outlook?

❒ Is any behavior holding you back from achieving your goals?

HEALTH AND PHYSICAL WELL-BEING:

❐ Do you want to lose weight? Gain weight?

❐ Do you want to eat right and exercise regularly?

❐ Do you want to lower your blood pressure? Develop six-pack abs?

RELATIONSHIPS:

❐ Do you want to meet someone?

❐ Do you want to get married?

❐ Do you want to be treated better?

HELPING OTHERS:

❐ Do you want to make the world a better place?

❐ Can you volunteer for an organization helping less fortunate people?

❐ Do you want to see your own special vision of philanthropy become a reality?

FUN AND RECREATION:

❐ How do you want to enjoy your free time?

❐ Is there something you have always wanted to do?

❐ If you did not have to work, how would you spend your waking hours?

❐ If money was not an issue, how would you choose to spend each day?

Make sure the goals you set are ones you legitimately want to achieve, not ones that other people might label as necessary to define success. In other words, be true to yourself. Don't create a goal of earning $10 million because society says that multimillionaires have it made. Success is not measured by your bank account. Everyone has a different definition of success, and success comes in many forms. Genuine success is an ongoing realization of your desired results and the satisfying achievement of your individual goals. To some that might mean becoming a better parent, while others might define it as climbing a mountain, living on a beach, earning a black belt, overcoming a disease or addiction, or becoming independently wealthy. Success depends on your perspective and what you value in life, not anyone else's idea or definition of success.

Write down, record, or type your big picture or lifetime goals. Keep it accessible because you will be revisiting it frequently.

If you have determined your final destination, it's time to work on the roadmap to get you there.

MISSED OPS:
High School Reunion

I didn't want to go to my ten-year high school reunion—what was the point? Anyone I wanted to see, I was still in touch with, and I'd be spending that the evening making awkward conversation or reminiscing about events I couldn't quite remember. I assumed Carolyn would feel the same, though when she told me she wanted to go, I wasn't surprised. She'd always been a social person, one of the most popular girls at our school.

"It's going to be fun, Henry," she said as we flew over some flat expanse of country that I'd never visited. Iowa, maybe. "Do you think anyone we went to school with would've thought we'd end up married?"

I smiled and conceded that she did have a point. It might sound like a dig at me, to word it that way, but she was right. Like I said, in high school, she was popular, and I was . . . well, less than popular would be putting it kindly. I'm sure if you'd asked anyone back then, they'd have bet all their money that someone like Carolyn would surely end up with the likes of Phil Snyder.

We came from a small town, and Phil was the guy who was going to put our small town on the map. He played all sports well, but he was truly gifted when it came to baseball. He could hit, he could pitch, and when he was in the lineup, we rarely lost a game.

I tried out for the team all four years and made it the last two. Technically, I only made it to the junior varsity team, but I got called up after several of the varsity players had to relinquish their spots because of injuries and academic probations. I knew everyone thought I would be nothing more than a glorified bat boy, but I honestly couldn't believe my good luck and resolved to do whatever I could to get some playing time. I thought that perhaps by being close to Phil I might absorb some talent through sheer osmosis.

But Phil rarely showed up for practice. I'd see him walking to the student parking lot, his girlfriend of the week in tow, when he should've been heading to the locker room. One time I found him taking a nap underneath the bleachers in the gymnasium. When he did come to practice, often he was late. Coach wasn't happy about it, but what could he do? So he'd just grit his teeth and say, "Snyder, how good of you to join us." He could never be too mad at Phil because he knew one day he'd see him playing in the majors, and maybe during some postgame interview, Phil would give his old high school coach a shout out, sing his praises.

Once at practice, Phil would stroll over to the batting cage, pick up a bat, take a few practice swings, and then hit any ball that was pitched to him: sliders, curveballs, split-finger fastballs, you name it. The only pitcher on the team able to throw a knuckleball was Phil, but everyone knew he'd be able to hit that one as well.

He made a rare appearance in the weight room one day. I was doing arm curls, thinking if I could bulk up my arms, I'd be able to throw harder and hit farther. I was concentrating on what I was doing, but at the same time, I was aware of Phil watching me. He continued to do so until I stopped and looked at him.

He smiled. "You know, you almost make that look fun."

I wiped the sweat from my forehead. "It's not so bad."

"Yeah, I was into it for a little while, but it gets boring pretty fast. And I can think of about, oh, a hundred other things I'd rather do first."

"We've got a big game coming up this weekend."

"I know." He tilted his head. "Are you in the lineup?"

"I don't know."

He nodded slowly. "I see. Well, I'll see you around." I watched as he ambled over to the soda machine in the corner, dropped some coins in, got a drink, and then ambled back out.

We won the game that weekend, though I didn't get to play. Phil hit a walk-off homerun in extra innings.

The reunion was held at JT's, the local restaurant/pub in the center of town. A large banner hung out front, welcoming our class.

"Guess we're in the right place," I said, and Carolyn tugged my arm, pulling me through the door.

The evening would have passed quite unremarkably, with me reiterating the same details over and over again: Yes, Carolyn and I were married. No, we didn't have any kids and weren't sure if we would. Yes, I owned two high-end restaurants that I started from scratch, didn't buy in to.

It was an open bar and I got another beer, stepped off to the side to take a breather, to have a minute alone. I looked toward the back of the restaurant and saw someone sitting by himself at a table tucked into the corner. It was easy for me to recognize him, though he looked completely different: his neck and waistline had both thickened and softened, his face was deeply lined, the hair at the front of his head had started to thin and recede. But there was still that hint of fluid motion as he picked up his beer bottle, took a sip, and placed it back down.

I walked over. "Hi, Phil."

He looked startled, though only for a second, and then his face broke out into a grin. He asked me how I was doing. I gave him the rundown and then asked the same of him. His smile faltered, but he started talking. He had two young children, with a third on the way. When his girlfriend got pregnant, he'd had to drop out of college and get a job on an excavating crew. He worked a few nights a week at a gas station convenience store, in part, he said, because they needed the money, but also because he needed a little time to himself.

"Nights are usually slow," he told me, picking at the label on the beer bottle. "It's nice. I can just sit back, put my feet up, and have a little relaxing time. I usually don't have more than half a dozen customers show up in a shift."

I smiled and struggled to think of something to say. The silence stretched. I looked over the room, searching for Carolyn. "Well," I said, "it was nice seeing you"

"You know, I think about you sometimes," he said as though he hadn't heard me. "How hard you used to work when we both played on the baseball team. You weren't even that good, and I don't think Coach put you in for more than three or four innings that whole season. But it didn't matter to you, did it? It didn't matter." He shook his head, as if in wonder. "And now to hear you've got two restaurants that are doing so well. I'm happy for you; I really am. I can only imagine how much work that was. Or is." He paused, though I could tell there was something else he needed to say. So I waited.

"I just . . . sometimes when I'm sitting at the store, or I'm at home trying to get one kid out of the bathtub and the other's screaming from her crib, I can't help but wonder how things might've been different for me if I had worked a little harder. If I had been a little more like you were. Maybe I could've played pro ball. Maybe I wouldn't be working sixty-hour weeks and still barely making enough money to put food on the table and pay the monthly rent to live in some dump. Maybe if I had worked a little harder you'd see me on ESPN or the cover of Sports Illustrated. I always thought that 'cause it came naturally, it would last. No one ever told me otherwise."

It was my turn to pause and wonder if I should say what popped into my head. I did, with the hope it might make him feel better, though I doubted it would. "I worked so hard at baseball because I wanted to be like you."

He looked at me incredulously. "That's why you worked so hard?"

I nodded. "One of the reasons, anyway."

"What were the others?"

"I . . . I don't know. I guess I just wanted to try to do my best—even if that meant never playing a full game—so I would know I did everything I could. And I wasn't any good; I knew that. But it was still kind of fun to imagine that maybe if I tried hard enough I might be half as good as you were."

"Yeah, well, I'm nothing anybody'd want to be now," Phil said, gazing at the neck of his beer bottle. "I can't stand to even look at myself in the mirror anymore because all I see is some fool who was more interested in girls and having fun. I used to miss practice to go hang out with Ashleigh Holbrook. Her parents were never home and they didn't care how many people she had over. It was a lot more fun than going to practice and doing drills and working out." He sighed and ran a hand through his thinning hair. "But what do I have to show for it now? I could be playing in the majors. I could be making a real nice living. People could still look at me and think, 'Now there's a guy I'd like to be like.' You don't still want to be like me, do you?"

I looked down at my shoes and tried to think of the least awkward way to extricate myself from the conversation.

"It's okay, you don't have to answer that," Phil went on. "I know I wasted pretty much every opportunity that ever presented itself to me just because having fun seemed like the better choice. At least in the short-term." He smiled and tipped his beer bottle to me. "Thanks for talking, Henry. It was nice to see you. Maybe if we ever make it out to California, we'll stop by one of your restaurants. Go to a baseball game."

"I'd like that," I said, though I knew it would never happen.

WHAT NOT TO DO:

❒ Become complacent or lazy because something comes easy to you.

ADVICE:
- ❐ Set goals and make a plan.
- ❐ Keep improving your skills and abilities; always strive to be the best, even if you aren't.
- ❐ Think of how your skills can get you what you want in life.

THE PLAN

Once you have your major lifetime goal set, it is time to outline a subset of progressively smaller goals. Start with those larger goals that are closest to your primary lifetime goal and work backward from there to the present moment. Each of your smaller goals should act as a rung on a ladder to help you reach your lifetime goals, and each of your goals should be based on first having reached a previous goal. Designing your plan this way enables you to see that your once seemingly unattainable lifetime goal is now realistic, and you can begin working on today, with the resources you already have at hand. While you're compiling your list of goals, you should have an "Aha!" moment when you say, "Wow, I really can do this!"

Once you have organized your outline, create a daily to-do list of tasks that will help you reach the first goal on your list. In the early stages, these daily projects may be, for example, to gather information, to begin training, or to get educated. For instance, if you want to start an import and export business, or maybe just travel to Europe, you might need to first learn a foreign language. Setting up a plan and outlining your short-term objectives will give you the ability to see and seize an opportunity when it arises.

SET EFFECTIVE GOALS
- ❐ Write down each goal: Post it in a visible spot and look at it daily.
- ❐ Be precise: Include dates, times, and a deadline for completion.
- ❐ Prioritize: Rank each goal by its priority.
- ❐ Keep smaller goals achievable: You will see results and progress, which will keep you motivated.

❐ Accept unpredictable circumstances: Life cannot be controlled, so do not feel bad if a goal fails for reasons beyond your control! Chalk it up and move forward.

SMART GOALS

Specific

Measurable

Attainable

Relevant

Time-bound

You, too, can determine what you want.
You can decide on your major objectives, targets, aims, and destination.

W. Clement Stone

STAYING ON COURSE

This next step, staying on course, is the most difficult. With life's unpredictable circumstances, it is tough to keep your goals in sight, to consistently work toward them, and all while remaining on track. Time is an asset you can never get back, and budgeting time is a battle we all wage, but there are practical ways you can fit in what you have to do without feeling rushed or overwhelmed.

Every day try to think of just one task you can focus on, and then work toward or complete it before you advance to your next goal. This will get you into a regular habit of being proactive, and soon you will be automatically fitting your "plan" into your busy schedule as you successfully navigate life's many surprises. It's been said that the way to eat an entire elephant is one small bite at a time. The same goes for managing your time and daily objectives on the way toward accomplishing a major lifetime goal.

Try to be flexible with your plan and the accompanying goals. Revisit your goals and modify them if need be to ensure that they are manageable. Being flexible and keeping an open mind will also invite more opportunities and open new doors. Modifying goals or even changing them completely is not a bad thing and may be necessary as life unfolds. Things change, and evolving to adapt to change is essential.

Chris wanted to own and operate a successful business, and he wanted the financial freedom to create his own work schedule. So he started his own clothing line tailored to a specific niche of teenagers and young adults who took part in the underground "rave" dance scene. He clearly defined his goals and worked toward them every day, but his business wasn't working out the way he had hoped or planned. Several years passed and Chris still wasn't gaining any more ground. He realized he had to make a change. He went back to his list of goals, tweaked a few, and changed the focus of his plan.

Chris recognized that within the industry many small clothing lines like his were paying huge amounts of money to have their pieces manufactured. Chris saw a glaring opportunity to coordinate and consolidate all their orders to ensure better quality at a lower wholesale price. Chris had also made an incredible number of valuable connections while trying to launch his clothing line. He contacted smaller clothing lines and collected orders from them. Then he arranged overseas manufacturing with a company that agreed to his terms.

Soon Chris was the proud and happy owner of a very successful clothing manufacturing brokerage business. Today many small businesses in that industry niche hire him to handle their clothing manufacturing needs. By keeping his goals flexible, Chris was able to recognize and take advantage of an opportunity he discovered while pursuing his goal. He didn't have to change his ultimate goal, which was to own and operate a successful business with his own hours and boatloads of money, he just needed to slightly modify his original plan to get there.

ACHIEVING GOALS

When you achieve a goal, reward yourself. Celebrate. Savor your success. Use that accomplishment to motivate you to reach your next goal. Evaluate and analyze how you achieved it, listing what you did right and what you could have done better. Reaching smaller, more incremental goals helps prepare you to tackle your larger ones. So honor those benchmarks and use every success or achievement to fuel your determination and push you closer to the attainment of a bigger goal or dream.

COPING WITH FAILURE

Missed Ops shows what some people do right and most people do wrong when opportunities come their way. Though we can't cover every opportunity one might face, because the possibilities are limitless, using the coaching tools we teach, you can easily adapt them to your unique situation and experiences, thus limiting your failure rate.

If you do fail to meet some of your goals, know that failing is part of goal setting. Learn from your mistakes and use them as motivation and practical guidance when you create your next set of goals. Develop the mind-set of getting as much from a failure as you do from a success and you will have a can-do attitude that nothing can possibly defeat. Get angry, get determined, get energized, or get excited. Do whatever works to push onward toward your next objective. The measure of one's character is not how hard he falls but how fast he gets back up.

Hard Work Alone Gets You No Where

- 4 -

The definition of hard work is exertion or effort that is difficult or challenging and is intended to produce a desired outcome. It is important to understand that all successful people put a tremendous amount of hard work into achieving their goals. And it is equally important to know that when you're faced with an opportunity and don't apply hard work to take full advantage of it, you will end up with regrets.

Initially, fifteen teams passed over football wide receiver Jerry Rice because they said he was too slow to play in the NFL. But Rice practiced so hard that other players got sick of trying to keep up with him. A thirteen-time Pro Bowl player, Rice is now in the NFL Hall of Fame as an all-time leader in several categories and is generally regarded as one of the best football players in history.

While writing this book, we asked many successful people to describe themselves in one word. The vast majority said "hardworking."

Why are so many successful people hard working? And why is challenge so important in becoming successful? Why not just choose the easiest route? The majority of the population chooses the easy way and the path of least resistance. Want proof? Just look at the middle and lower economic echelons of society. They constitute the largest population of people. If the majority takes the easier path and winds up at the bottom of the heap, that is specifically why you should do the opposite.

Plenty of phony get-rich-quick schemes are promoted as the opportunity of a lifetime. And there are just as many people who will seek the easiest path to what they want in life. It is usually these underachievers who are targeted by scams that promise overnight success. But those people typically end up with nothing more than a ton of regret and frustration. I know because I used to be one of them.

I started business after business, looking for a way to become wealthy fast. Failed venture after failed venture taught me many lessons, but the most important thing I learned is that hard work is a prerequisite to success. Anything you want in life can be yours, but nothing will come your way until you invest hard work.

Being healthy takes hard work. Following a daily workout plan when you'd rather be watching television or taking a nap isn't easy. Dieting when you'd rather eat everything on the menu takes willpower, and that's work. Maintaining a positive relationship can require strenuous effort. Ask any marriage counselor. They will tell you marriage is work because both parties have to compromise and accept their partner's differences and diligently stay committed to each other. Rearing kids is really hard work. Sacrificing time and postponing plans of your own for the needs and wants of your children takes energy and constant sacrifice. Setting goals and following your plans to achieve them is hard work. Making a daily effort to examine your progress and stay on track requires self-discipline.

But here's the kicker. What many people fail to realize is that not putting 100 percent effort into getting what they want is also extremely strenuous.

Think about how much effort it takes to do something if you can't stand doing. How hard is it to drag yourself to a job you hate or stay in a relationship that makes you miserable? Not doing anything to change your circumstances for the better and reach your heartfelt goals demands a tremendous amount from you. In the long run, taking the so-called "easy route" is often much harder than people perceive.

As long as you have to work hard and endure difficulties in life, why not choose to do it in pursuit of your own goals? If you focus additional effort on reaching your goals, you will get where you want to be. During your journey, the hard work it takes to get there will also feel less like work because you're following your own path to achieve your dreams.

How long will you slumber, O sluggard?
When will you rise from your sleep?

A little sleep, a little slumber,
A little folding of the hands to sleep—
So shall your poverty come on you like a prowler.

Proverbs 6:9–11

BECOME A HARD WORKER

Here is a post found on an Internet blogging site, written by a teenager looking for help to become a harder worker:

> Help! I wanna become a hard worker, but I'm such a lazy bum.

I'm so lazy, have no self-discipline what-so-ever, and give up on almost anything that I start in a few seconds. I really don't want to end up as one of those losers who is living in their parents basement . . . and my grades suck, too. I can't get organized to save my life, and I can't start a "routine" that should help me get organized for more than an hour. I just get so lost in the middle of it all. I wish I were one of those hardworking people who don't give up for anything. I really have to get my life in order before it's too late!

Many of us won't consider ourselves at this level of extreme laziness. But if by chance you do, or if some of this teen's frustration sounds familiar, then take out your highlighter and start paying attention.

As for me, I can relate to how that teenage blogger feels because I wasn't always a hard worker. In elementary school I was a mediocre student with average grades. In junior high and high school, school became more difficult and my grades suffered even more. I was always looking for the easy way out, and I was a dreamer with very little work ethic to back it up. I would spend more time thinking of ways to forge the grades or signatures on my report cards than I would spend studying for tests or doing homework assignments. At home my parents had to nag me to do my chores and then I would procrastinate as long as I could before doing them halfheartedly. I was a slacker by every definition of the word. It wasn't until later in life that I started to realize how important hard work is in every aspect of life.

If being a hard worker does not come naturally for you, you can change your habits and beliefs to achieve a high level of willpower. Once you have that you will be motivated from within to consistently pursue your dreams. You can change if you want something bad enough.

Laziness travels so slowly that poverty soon overtakes him.

Benjamin Franklin

Do Something You Love

What are you interested in? It could be anything. Write down everything you can do with that particular interest. Include how far you can take it. Make a list of goals from largest to smallest.

Let's say your interest is related to video games. You might start your list of goals by writing "I want to become a professional video game player. "Next list several smaller goals, such as "I will place in a local tournament," or "I will beat my friend ten times in a row."

Now approach your goal as if it were a daily job until you reach some of the smaller goals or rungs on your achievement ladder. Do this to the best of your ability and keep at it. The thing you love to do will become work, and you are going to put 100 percent effort into it. Make a schedule for yourself, as many hours you can spare a day, and don't deviate from it. When you don't feel like doing it, push yourself a little further each time.

Working at something you are interested in or passionate about will be easier than doing something you don't enjoy. By using something you love to motivate you and working hard at it, you trick yourself into learning self-discipline. Once you master that, you will know how to work hard at anything else in life. Self-discipline to consistently work at something can be applied to any other situation, and it will empower you to reach all your goals.

When we talk about "vocation," we usually mean a job or career, whereas "avocation" normally refers to a hobby. Jerry Rice liked playing football, an avocation in his young life, but he turned it into a vocation by making a career out of something he loved to do for fun and recreation. You may be able to do the same thing with whatever it is you enjoy doing in your spare time.

Mike Francesa and Chris Russo from Mike and the Mad Dog radio show turned their interest into a career. They weren't athletic like Jerry Rice; like most of us they preferred to watch sports instead of getting out on the field and competing. But they put a lot of hard work into what they loved doing. While watching sporting events, they weren't passive. They worked at it by taking notes and studying players, coaches, and strategies to learn as much as they could. While other people slumped on the sofa, watching the game, Russo and Francesa put all their effort into studying the game—and figured out how to turn their passion and dream into a successful career.

I always liked working out with weights in the gym. But it was a casual hobby. I did it sometimes and at other times I was just not really into it that much. All I knew was that I liked going to the gym with friends and lifting weights.

Then one day a college classmate was talking about some bodybuilding shows in which he competed. The whole class circled around him as he intrigued them with his stories and pictures. Even the teacher became enamored. This bodybuilder noticed that I worked out, and being friendly he asked if I wanted to do a show with him six months from now. I hesitated, but my peers and even my professor pressured me, so I eventually and reluctantly agreed. About twenty people from school said they were coming to this show, so I thought, "What did I get myself into?"

I wasn't a bodybuilder and I didn't even like to get up in front of the class and speak, let alone stand in a pair of Speedos before hundreds of strangers. But I wanted to be prepared and not humiliated, so from that point on, my social hobby turned into a full-time obsession.

I read books and magazines, surfed the Internet, watched videos, and talked to people at the gym. I absorbed anything that would help me get ready. Fear motivated me—fear of embarrassment and failure—but is was enough to push me to eat bland diet foods and hit the gym for hours each day. My friends partied while I stayed home and slept so I could get up early and do cardio before the gym. At family gathering my relatives ate huge servings of Italian food while I dined on egg whites and lettuce.

But the experience taught me the true meaning of hard work, sacrifice, and self-discipline. I took first place in that show and accomplished more than I set out to do. It was all thanks to the amount of effort I put into my "hobby." That is how I conditioned myself to apply the hard work ethic. After that I could adapt it to any other goal or aspect of my life. Remember that hard work is necessary to achieve anything worthwhile.

Do unto Others

While it may sound strange, helping others usually makes us feel better about ourselves. It doesn't matter how small or insignificant a task may seem to you, because to those people who need help it is definitely important. So help them to the best of your ability. Ask your wife or parents what tasks need to be done around the house. Ask coworkers if they need help with a project or even carrying something out to their cars. Ask a person changing a flat tire if you can help. Ask friends if they need help painting the fence or washing their cars.

Do your best while helping others and it will condition you to work harder in other areas of your own life. Your mind will start to associate the good feelings of helping others with how it feels to work hard at a personal need.

Learn from Example

If you don't have a mentor or someone who gives you sound, objective guidance, that's fine. You can just as easily learn from other people's positive habits. Work ethic is easily learned during childhood from adults we admire and respect. If you weren't fortunate enough to have someone like that around when you were growing up, that is okay; it is not too late to start learning. If you look up to or admire someone, you tend to model or imitate some of their behaviors. Choose a person—a successful business owner, a parent, or anyone else you admire—who is where you want to be and ask her how she got there. If you cannot find someone you can talk to, choose one or two people from books, magazines, or the Internet. Do some research on the person, read his success stories, and identify how he got where you want to be. After gathering information on that person, pick out his good work habits and emulate them. If you've chosen successful people, I would be willing to bet that they used hard work to get where they are. People aren't born with predispositions to become successful; they use hard work and experience to achieve their goals.

Ask not what your company can do for you, but what you can do for your company.

Whether or not you like your job (or school) is irrelevant when training to become a hard worker. Start conditioning yourself to do more than is required of you at your place of business or school. What can you do above and beyond your daily tasks? Can you help increase profit margins, improve the morale of your coworkers, or even make your workplace a neater or nicer place to work? Put some extra effort into your daily routine. To become a hard worker you have to balance a self-focused tenacity or drive with an eagerness to do more than is expected. Conditioning yourself to do more than what is required will help you to become a hard worker. This habit will not only make you stand out among your coworkers, but your superiors and others will take notice and label you a hard worker, which can also open more doors of opportunity.

Be Healthy

Hard work takes energy, but being healthy helps you feel better and work harder without being tired, run down, or sick. Take good care of your body and mind. Get on an exercise program because working out daily will help you focus on your goals, and feeling physically better will give you the energy you need to pursue them. Studies show that exercising increases blood flow to the brain, and increased blood flow means more oxygen and nutrients, which in turn translate into better cognitive function.

During a study done by Duke University in 1999, researchers found that daily exercise led to significant improvements in memory, planning, and organizational functions, in addition to increasing the ability to mentally juggle different intellectual tasks at the same time. James Blumenthal, a Duke psychologist and the study's principal investigator, stated that exercise has beneficial effects in specific areas of cognitive function that are rooted in the frontal and prefrontal regions of the brain.[6] An increase in these cognitive or mental functions means you will be more alert and more keenly aware of opportunities—opportunities you might have missed had you not been getting your regular dose of physical exercise.

Follow a healthy diet. The brain performs countless functions and requires continuous energy to carry out its tasks. Improving your diet can increase your mental function both directly and indirectly by supplying a steady stream of nutrients your brain needs, while enhancing cognitive strength along with your overall health. A research paper published by Goldman and Morris in 2001 explained that their clinical study showed that healthy people did not experience memory impairment as much as they aged.[7] Following a healthy diet will not only increase brain function but also help prevent mental decline.

After exercise and diet comes mental health and emotional wellness as the third critical component to being healthy. Set aside quality time to spend with family and friends. Have a good time and relax. Use your vacation time even if you don't go anywhere, and don't let work be your only source of enjoyment. Take care of your emotional, spiritual, and romantic needs and desires. Dr. John Gottman's research found that emotional awareness and the ability to handle feelings determine our success and happiness in all walks of life and in our family relationships, even more than IQ or intelligence does.

If At First You Don't Succeed, Try Again . . . and Again!

Do not give up. Willpower is the ability to do something even when you don't feel like it. When you achieve that level of willpower to do what is hard, you gain access to a sense of self-discipline that will keep you moving forward when things get rough. The willingness to do what is difficult leads to feelings of euphoria when you have completed a challenging task. Use self-discipline and willpower to persevere, because hard workers don't give up when the going gets tough. Your self-satisfying can-do attitude will help strengthen and enhance the other positive skills you have already been practicing.

Reward Yourself

Give yourself a reward—a day off, a trip somewhere fun, or some new clothes—but only if and when you deserve it. At the end of the week make a list of all the tasks you completed beyond the call of duty. Note that I did not say tasks started. Hard workers finish what they set out to accomplish. Review the list. Are you are satisfied by what you achieved that week?

You can't put a set number of how many completed tasks add up to deserving a reward, though, because everyone is different, with unique lives and responsibilities. I suggest that you simply use the number of tasks pertaining to your goals as a general point of reference. If you accomplished enough to deserve your reward, you will know it in your gut. Be honest with yourself and accept rewards only for work that really matters. But if you feel you earned it, then celebrate and congratulate yourself.

If what I completed this week is greater than last week's number, I will reward myself. I opt for other rewards rather than taking a whole day to relax and do nothing. Being conditioned through years of hard work makes it difficult to be inactive and unproductive. Hard work becomes infectious. Sitting around doing nothing after you have done so much makes you feel like you're wasting time, so be sure to give yourself adequate time to unwind or you will soon get burned out. But when you reach that point where you are willing to keep working and have to discipline yourself to take it easy once in a while, you will know you have become a genuine hard worker.

Keep Progressing

Once you understand how to increase your willpower and self-discipline and have started to work your hardest all the time, keep moving in that direction. Keep practicing these fundamental skills until you have proven to yourself that you are a hard worker who motivates yourself to keep persevering, no matter what.

Believe in yourself. Anyone can be a hard worker!

HARDWORKING, MISERABLE PEOPLE

Now that you know how to define hard work and how to become a hard worker, it is time to tell you how hard work alone will get you nowhere. Hard work is, of course, commonly connected with strong results—but not all by itself. If hard work is so great and self-satisfying, why are there so many hardworking, miserable people in the world? Look at the faces of people commuting to work each morning in subways, buses, and cars. Throughout my various career paths, I've encountered many hardworking people from all walks of life. I have to say that most of those people wallowed in their misery. They were miserable about their jobs, home lives, kids, parents, and coworkers. These kinds of people complain about everything, and their negative energy is enough to suck the life from any room.

So why then do so many experts say that hard work leads to happiness? Researchers from Gothenburg University in Sweden analyzed published data on what makes people genuinely happy, and they concluded that working to achieve a goal makes people more satisfied than working without a goal.[8]

Hard work can lead to happiness only if your hard work brings you what you want. Working hard without personal rewards and achievements becomes a grind, an endless road to nowhere. If you go to work, put in all your effort, come home, eat, sleep, wake up, and head back to work again without achieving any of your personal goals, you are spinning your wheels. If you're in a rat race that has no end, it's time for a change. It's time to realize you need more than just hard work to become successful and happy. Get off the treadmill and onto a path toward fulfillment of your goals and dreams.

Growing up I was surrounded by close family members who worked hard in their various careers. But they never seemed to be happy. They worked very hard for their families, just as they were raised to do. They put in countless extra hours and had second jobs in addition to their demanding duties at home.

My mother was the hardest working school teacher I knew. She stayed up late every night grading papers and writing lesson plans. The neighborhood recognized her as one of the best teachers in the district. All the kids liked her, and all the parents wanted her to teach their children. For thirty-five years straight she went to work, tutored after school, and took care of her family at home—in addition to doing laundry, cooking, and cleaning. But despite her dedication to her students and devotion to her children, she was not a happy person.

My grandfather is another example of a hard worker. A World War II veteran, he worked twenty-five years for the NYPD and then retired and immediately started working construction. After his body wouldn't let him do that any longer, he started a third career as a security guard. While working those jobs, he also helped family and friends with home improvement projects. I never saw him sitting around doing nothing during his waking hours. But despite all his activity and productivity, he trudged through life under a cloud of personal melancholy.

Humans are peculiar creatures. For one reason or another we are more than willing to put up with misery, and we are extremely reluctant to change for the better.

My mother and grandfather were like so many others in this world: hard workers with no sense of direction when it came to fulfilling their own dreams. They never set long-term goals and never talked about what their dreams were. They never received any guidance on becoming successful. They only knew how to keep their mouths shut and work hard for the benefit of others. If you have only some of the habits of a highly effective person but have no hope of ever seeing a personal goal rewarded, it is hard to maintain momentum and motivation. Dream big, because hard work alone will get you nowhere.

MISSED OP:
Young and Misguided

While making my way through high school and college, my most definitive quality was my industriousness. I was willing to work day and night for money, and was not inclined to shy away from any opportunity. When my older brother was seventeen, he proposed starting a landscaping business, and I was eager to get involved. My two brothers and I—we were all very close in age—joined together in a feat that showcased the energy and vitality of youth and built a business that, had its construction been coupled with planning and foresight, could have made all of us a lot of money and made my teenage dreams come true. The business had rather humble beginnings, to say the least. Using our bicycles, we transported the tools of our trade—a three-horsepower Jacobson lawnmower, a gas can, and a broom—from lawn to lawn. Through diligent, hard work and very low prices, we acquired about ten loyal customers over the first year. As our business continued to grow, we gradually upgraded our lawn equipment to more impressive, commercial models. Hungry for more success, we also started an aggressive advertising campaign, plastering our flyers all over the houses, car windshields, and grocery store bulletin boards of the surrounding neighborhoods. Everyone within a fifteen mile radius knew that we would be more than happy to mow their lawns. Before anyone, including ourselves, knew it, we had over a hundred accounts that spanned five local towns, and a business with a great reputation. That's not too bad for a few hard-working kids in their late teens and early twenties who'd started with bicycles and a residential-sized mower.

Building that business came with many benefits; at least, that was how we saw it. We earned excellent money, which helped us build up a remarkable amount of equity; in addition, we stayed in good physical shape and got great tans (working outside for thirteen hours every day). Best of all, we were our own men. We had our own business, which allowed us to make decisions for ourselves, employ people, and feel a strong sense of freedom. Despite all that potential, I remained stuck in the moment. I never asked myself if I wanted to be a landscaper for the rest of my life, or if there was a way to use this business to get closer to achieving any goal I might set. More important, no one ever sat me down and talked to me about all the ways in which this business could have been a great tool for me to get where I wanted to go.

Everyone in my advice pool—parents, siblings, relatives, friends, customers, business associates—neglected to step in to ask me what I was expecting to do with this business in the long term. They never asked me what I wanted from it, or even sought to remind me that there was potential in the business I had worked so hard to build, that it contained other possibilities and opportunities. In the end, my lack of guidance as a young man with a large amount of expendable income led me to squander my money on transient pleasures like vacations, cars, and girls. I often think of all the possibilities I missed, and what I could have done if I had the opportunity to do it over.

WHAT NOT TO DO:
- ❐ Work hard without any short- and long-term goals.

ADVICE:
- ❐ Ask successful business people what to do with your new-found money.
- ❐ Seek wisdom outside your advice pool.
- ❐ Have a plan in place for your future goals.

OPPORTUNITY + EXPERIENCE + HARD WORK = SUCCESS

Success isn't handed to us; it requires a lot of hard work. Yet that isn't enough, because many people work hard for decades without becoming successful. One must ask, what exactly is missing?

Opportunity

Somewhere in the formula for success, you need an opportunity. You need an opportunity to get your screenplay made into a movie, to meet your future wife or husband, to receive or make a business proposal, to get a job offer, to go to school, to invest, to try out for a sports team, to sell your invention, or to get your book published. Every successful person has encountered an opportunity at one time or another. Be mindful that opportunities are all around us. It is up to us to recognize them. As mentioned in Chapter 1, if you have a difficult time seeing opportunities, try to surround yourself with creative people, write down problems (no matter how small they may seem), listen to outrageous outside-the-box ideas, and organize group brainstorming meetings. Keep your eyes, ears, and mind open to possibilities around you, and you can discover or create the opportunities you need to reach your ultimate goal.

Experience

First, you must gain knowledge and experience—your own or someone else's. Without experience you will not know what decisions to make without taking risks and leaving the outcome to random chance. If you don't have a vast amount of experience in taking advantage of opportunities, your next best option is to learn from others who do.

A mentor is someone who has knowledge and experience with something you are striving for and steers you toward your goal. A good mentor is part teacher, part role model, and part advisor. Having a mentor is a great way to learn what it takes to succeed in your life's chosen path or current profession. Mentors guide you so you can make better decisions as you pursue your goals. Use their experiences as your own.

If you don't know someone who would be a good mentor, find one on the Internet. A couple of useful websites help connect people to well-established mentors from various industries. If you don't want a personal mentor, find mentoring resources like this book, seminars, networking functions, the Internet, or just conversations with people who can share lessons learned from their mistakes and achievements.

Remember that experience is the best teacher, and the quickest and simplest way to become successful is by using other people's experiences as if they were your own. Use other people's experiences to avoid common pitfalls and keep you moving in a positive, progressive direction with fewer setbacks and less need for trial and error or experimentation. Remember that franchising is a successful business model built on this same concept.

Hard Work

Once you have gained the experience you need and discovered what opportunities are available, the final element of the success formula is hard work—the glue that fuses experience and opportunity together. It's the catalyst that ignites achievement and the fuel that keeps the fire of motivation and success burning brightly.

The wonderful thing about hard work is that it's universal. It doesn't matter what your opportunities are, because hard work can be used to leverage them into positive results, regardless of your goals. Being a hard worker will ensure you are consistently moving toward your goals with energy and diligence, even when things aren't easy. Hard work can level an uneven playing field and create opportunities that didn't exist before. And once you achieve success, your hard work will ensure your ability to maintain it and expand upon it in a sustainable, satisfying way.

Let's say, for example, that John wants to open a restaurant. He gains all the experience necessary, reads informative books, interviews successful business owners and other mentors, studies the competition, and analyzes markets, trends, and locations. Then an opportunity presents itself to John. A storefront comes for sale at an affordable price in a perfect location with lots of foot traffic. John puts together a staff and opens his doors for business. But John lacks the hard work it takes to launch, manage, and continually operate his business. His restaurant fails. He has two of the three components of the success formula, but one important key is missing: his own contribution of hard work.

Remove any element of the formula and the equation works out the same way. Say John works hard and gains all the experience necessary, but that opportunity never materializes and he fails to create one. He never even gets the chance to open the restaurant. And if John grabs the opportunity and works hard at running his restaurant, but he never gains the necessary business or restaurant industry experience, his restaurant venture will surely fail.

Every now and again someone will get lucky and become successful despite their lack of experience or hard work, but the one absolutely vital component that cannot be removed is opportunity. Without the right opportunity there can be no success because there is no situation to take advantage of until opportunity comes along.

The bottom line is that you need more than hard work alone to become successful. But you can achieve your dreams and goals when you use the right skills and success elements combined with the invaluable asset of your own hard work.

Great things are not done by impulse,
but by a series of small things brought together.

Vincent Van Gogh

Aim at More Than One Target and You Might Not Hit Any

–5–

Visualizing dreams sounds easy. It also seems easy to think about what you want in life and see yourself achieving it. Setting goals for yourself also appears simple. But establishing manageable goals and working to consistently achieve them is not nearly as easy as one might think, and it doesn't happen as effortlessly as many self-improvement or motivational books would have us believe.

Setting a goal might be relatively easy to do, but creating a process that helps you move toward achieving that objective takes greater effort. The key to successfully mastering this potentially frustrating and complicated goal-setting business is to focus on one goal at a time.

Focus is the ability to center your interest and action on a single isolated task, idea, or thought. When you focus, you direct your full attention to whatever it is you are trying to achieve. But that is easier said than done in this modern era of high-tech distractions.

Here's the important thing to remember: If you focus on too many things at one time, you will usually end up missing all of them. Try to shoot all the soda cans off of a fence with your BB gun in just one shot and you probably won't hit any cans. Choose one target at a time, concentrate on it alone, and then squeeze the trigger before moving to the next target.

New scientific research into multitasking shows that people who do several things at one time don't do any of them particularly well. Their cognitive abilities such as memory and analytical thinking are also diminished.[9]

Not capitalizing on opportunities is a problem that transcends time. Our parents and their parents and grandparents missed opportunities because they spread their focus too thin. If you want to capitalize on opportunities, select your goals one at a time. People who master the art of hitting one nail with the hammer can build an entire house, but even a master carpenter will fail and look completely foolish if he or she tries to hit several nails all at once.

Concentrate all your thoughts upon the work at hand.
The sun's rays do not burn until brought to a focus

Alexander Graham Bell

FIVE CATEGORIES OF MENTAL FOCUS

Let's explore five categories of mental focus as they relate to lifetime goals. (Take your list of goals you wrote from Chapter 3, and refer to them as you read this chapter.)

Focus is essential if you want to achieve anything in life. Not only should we have focus, but we should know how to effectively apply it each step of the way to achieve our ultimate goals.

Lifetime Focus

Your lifetime focus should be to visualize your dreams and pursue them until they become a reality. But first ask yourself: "What is my lifetime focus?" Once you arrive at the answer, say it aloud and write it down to make it more tangible, visible, and real.

Remember, this is your dream not what your parents want you to be or something that conforms to social norms. If it doesn't sound sincere when you say it, or it doesn't look right on paper when you write it down, it probably lacks authenticity. So keep working at it until you nail down the true dream and goal that resonates with you and inspires your passion.

Is your heartfelt goal to become a company CEO? Find your soul mate? Be a millionaire? Travel the world? Get straight As? Launch your own charity as a philanthropist or humanitarian? Perform to sold-out audiences?

Whatever it may be, the hardest of these five categories is consistently focusing on your lifelong dreams and goals, because they are the farthest away from where you are when you first set them. They are like the archery target set so far away that you cannot yet see it from where you stand, so instead you have to try to visualize those long-range dreams and keep a picture of them in your mind's eye.

But you will be encouraged along the way, because achieving the smaller tasks and short-term goals that bring your big dream closer to reality is emotionally rewarding. Those profound feelings of self-satisfaction, pride, and personal happiness grow deeper with every new accomplishment, and your life becomes more fulfilling because it has purpose both in the short term and over the long haul.

Most people lack that kind of intentional direction in life. They never attain their dreams but instead settle for less and feel lousy and regretful because of it. Visualize your dreams. Concentrate on reaching them by daily focusing on them. Mediate on them the way a kicker in a clutch NFL game thinks about putting the ball through the uprights to win the Super Bowl.

The kicker doesn't show up out of nowhere to be a champion. He trains for that moment all his life, day in and day out. The smaller accomplishments in his football career, all the way back to junior high school, have been little goals and small victories that were necessary to allow him the rare opportunity to reach this major lifetime goal.

Stay motivated and keep working in a progressive, positive direction. Frequently ask yourself how the opportunities you've encountered you fit into the bigger scheme of things to enable you to seize your dream and call it your own. For example, if one of your lifetime goals is to travel the world, and a career change becomes available to you, calculate whether that opportunity will bring you closer to your dream or pull you away from it. Might the new job involve overseas journeys? Or could it tether you to one office and limit your ability to live out your dreams?

When I was younger and still single I worked as a waiter at the local Marriott hotel. I became a waiter to work my way up in the company to a high-level management position. I was willing to pay my dues and learn all aspects of the job, from the ground up. I broke down my goals. I implemented a plan. I was willing to do whatever it took to attain my managerial job. I worked hard and did more than was asked of me. But, admittedly, it was a slow process, I lost focus, and wound up taking a detour.

Next thing I knew I had reached another of my goals by becoming a Special Agent. But to this day I regret not having lived on a tropical isle, because my biggest dream was to live in an island paradise surrounded by a blue ocean with the sand outside my door and palm trees on the horizon.

Granted, I did wind up working in law enforcement and living on an island, so part of my agenda was fulfilled; however, it was not in the tropics but on the island of Manhattan, which is basically an overpopulated concrete jungle with long winters and skyscrapers instead of tropical breezes and palm trees.

The experience taught me to be careful and focus on specifics when working toward lifetime goals and dreams.

Multi-Year Focus

After establishing your lifetime focus, next is the multi-year focus, which is focusing on what will bring you very close to your ultimate dream, not totally, but that which is measurable and large enough to warrant several years of effort.

Let's say, for example, that your dream is to retire as a millionaire. You may want to create a multiyear goal of socking away half a million bucks by a certain time. Maybe you're a varsity football player whose dream is to play in a Super Bowl. But first you have a multiyear plan to attend college on a football scholarship, play well enough to get the attention of professional scouts, and get drafted into the NFL.

The idea is to concentrate on your lifetime goal, whatever that may be, while also focusing on a compatible and relevant multiyear goal.

Annual Focus

The annual focus is a one-year goal to bring you closer to your multiyear goal and ultimately your lifetime dream. But this one-year goal should be more specific than your multiyear goal and be both measurable and attainable.

Your annual goal should be revisited and focused on each day because unless you constantly remind yourself what you are working toward, it is too easy to lose focus. Keep this goal playing in the back of your mind all the time, like a theme song, to inspire you forward through the daily grind.

One, two, or maybe three goals per year is all you should have in front of you to keep focused enough to achieve all of them. Because these are relatively short-range targets, annual goals can be changed without risk of losing focus on your lifetime goal.

If your goal is to become a CEO, your yearly goal might be to get a promotion within the next 365 days. Or maybe your annual goal is to find a successful CEO to be your career mentor. You might need several yearly goals to reach your multiyear focus, so choose these annual goals with that bigger, multiyear target in mind. By achieving one or several multiyear goals, you will reach your lifetime focus.

Weekly Focus

To stay focused on a weekly level, set a goal at the beginning of each week and work to complete it before the week is over. Revisit the steps to achieve one of your smaller goals we outlined earlier. Review your goal, making daily notes, and try to meet your deadline, but don't be hard on yourself if you cannot complete your goal each week. Just roll it over to next week's goals but make sure it is completed.

It is okay if something takes more time than anticipated as long as you complete it before you shift your focus on the next goal. Weekly goals can be a few or many, depending on your responsibilities and how busy you are. Just be sure not to bite off more than you can chew. The more goals you work on at one time, the greater the risk that you will lose focus. Your weekly goals should always complement one another and point directly toward the yearly goal.

If your goal is to find the perfect husband or wife, your weekly focus might be to line up one or more dates by the following weekend. One goal may be to ask someone out on a date. Then plan your date with the idea to learn more about your potential mate. That planning and subsequent date can lead to another goal. In this way all the goals feed one another, with the ultimate long-range goal in mind and in focus.

Daily Focus

Here is where we focus on the things we will do for a day to achieve our weekly goals. What will help you achieve your next immediate goal? Prioritize daily tasks, taking a few minutes to write down what you want to accomplish before bedtime. At the top of your list should be the one task that will enable you to make the most progress toward reaching your weekly goal.

After you make your list of goals for the day, focus on each one separately until it is completed. Do not multitask; instead, try to prevent any distractions that may prevent you from achieving your daily goal.

Visualize yourself in all five categories.

Lacking visualization regarding one goal can decrease your overall performance on the rest of your goals, because they all work together as a cohesive plan. Seeing is believing, and to believe in your goals and dreams you need to see them all clearly. But picturing all five focus categories consistently takes practice and is a skill that takes time to master.

Daily visualization on all the categories will also invite unexpected opportunities, because working toward goals as you visualize them opens up your conscious awareness as well as your subconscious mind, making you more alert to opportunity. Visualize each goal and one day you'll wake up and realize that you are living your lifelong dream.

WHY WE FAIL AT MENTAL FOCUS

Our daily routines and habits hinder us from learning the skills we need to become successful. Every day we can think of reasons not to get focused or stay focused on what is most important to us. We have many competing interests. We are easily distracted. We don't like to say no when asked to do something for someone else. Some days we don't have much energy, or we get sick, which throws us off our stride. Maybe we haven't spent sufficient time thinking strategically about the process to achieve our goals, or perhaps we are just caught up in the day-to-day grind.

Stop and ask yourself, "Am I where I want to be in all areas of my life?" If not, the reason is probably because you lack concrete goals and adequate focus. If we spent as much time on those things as we do watching television, we would enjoy a great deal more success in life.

We know mental focus is necessary for peak performance, but still we spend very little time practicing to master it. Just like any other skill, mental focus takes time to develop. Let's say you have a goal to be a more efficient batter. If you practice swinging a bat every day, it is reasonable to assume that your batting average would increase. Practice playing scales on the piano every day and you'll be a more skilled pianist. The same can be said about your mental focus. Additionally, if you don't use it, you lose it.

If you learn the skills to increase mental focus and you do not consistently apply them to situations, you will never master them. Even after completing a task successfully, you do not automatically gain mental focus. That has to be nurtured on its own. Many people falsely think that they naturally acquire mental focus simply by practicing a physical skill over and over. But focus comes only by repeatedly training that unique neurological, psychological, or cognitive skill.

Another reason we fail to master focus is because we don't spend enough time mentally practicing. Part of mentally rehearsing a goal or task is to visualize doing it or accomplishing it.

In fact many experts believe that the brain doesn't know the difference between an imagined you and the real you; therefore, it is important to visualize yourself doing a task perfectly and confidently, reacting to every action. Your brain will perceive that image as the real you being successful, which will help you get into that magical and empowering zone.

ONE TARGET AT A TIME

When Anthony and I received firearms training at the FBI and DEA academies, we were told to focus each bullet on one shot and one target at a time. After each hit or miss on the range, we had to refocus, aim again, and fire. Our instructors drilled this practice into us for hours every day for sixteen straight weeks, which made it clear to us how important focus is.

These firing range principles can be applied to goals and opportunities. If we pursue too many goals at once, we risk missing all of them. The same can be said for long-term goals. Spreading your attention and focus over many goals will dilute your concentration, and you'll inevitably fail to reach some of them if not all of them.

Remember, if you aim at multiple targets at the same time, you probably won't hit any of them. Hammer one nail at a time as you construct your dreams and you'll build solid, faster results.

Most people have no idea of the giant capacity we can immediately command when we focus all of our resources on mastering a single area of our lives.

Tony Robbins

READY . . . AIM . . . FIRE!

Have you ever felt overwhelmed when trying to accomplish several things at once? If so, here's a hint: use the phrase Ready . . . Aim . . . Fire! whenever you approach tasks or opportunities.

Ready means just that. Be ready or prepared for the opportunity. Your experience and knowledge are the tools you need to get ready. Aim is focusing on one step at a time, breaking your larger goals down into smaller ones that you can easily focus on. Fire is the signal to take action. Once you are adequately prepared and focused, don't hesitate or procrastinate but go ahead and pull the trigger. Push your fears and apprehension aside and don't be too critical of yourself. Just take the first step and move forward. Once you have momentum, you can adapt or adjust. But you have to start; otherwise, you'll never get anywhere.

Some experts actually suggest acting in a different order: Ready . . . Fire . . . Aim! They believe it's more important to move forward before focusing on the target.

The validity of that argument can be debated, but the main thing is that either approach is a whole lot better than taking no action at all, remaining stagnant as opportunities pass you by.

If you don't get ready, take aim, and then fire, you are shooting blindfolded. You'll probably run out of ammo resources, motivation, confidence, opportunities, and time before you get anywhere near the target.

PRIORITIZE

Prioritizing identifies which tasks have greater importance at any given moment, allowing you to put more focus, effort, and time into them. You may have to set aside tasks of lesser value to focus on high-priority tasks that have greater benefit to you.

Have your list of goals or presented opportunities in front of you. Then use them to help list the things you want to accomplish every day, leading up to your larger weekly, monthly, yearly, and lifelong objectives. Rank them, assign them priority, based on the following factors.

Time Limitations

Break down your tasks according to time limits or deadlines. Decide which have to be done immediately and which need to be done within days, weeks, months, or years. Those that have the most immediate deadlines should be given top priority.

Pros and Cons

Compare the positives and negatives of each task. Study the task and connect it with your goal or opportunity. The tasks with the biggest positive-to-negative ratio should receive priority.

Weigh the Consequences

Evaluate the consequences of not doing something on your list. The ones that carry heavier consequences should get higher priority than the ones of lesser impact. Consequences vary with individuals and situations, so ask yourself, "What consequences can I live with? Which ones can I not tolerate?"

Weeding Out Junk

If you can eliminate mundane or unimportant tasks, do so. Delegating tasks to others and asking for help are two great ways to eliminate things you have to do. The less you have to do, the more time you can spend on the more important and profitable activities.

FOCUS ON POTENTIAL OPPORTUNITY

When dealing with opportunities, focus is one of the most important skills you need to be successful. If you think an opportunity is coming your way, focus on it until it reveals itself, or until you determine it is not feasible or worth chasing. List the pros and cons of pursuing this opportunity. Ask yourself what the chances are that it will actually happen and whether the opportunity fits with your other goals and aspirations. What will you have to sacrifice to achieve it? If the positives outweigh the negatives, then go for it. Outline what you'll have to do to achieve it, do the research, ask expert advice, and start working toward it.

MISSED OP:
Inventor

William was an aspiring inventor who continually looked for ways to get into the financial position he desired. He had a creative mind and often thought up new ways to make money. One day William created an opportunity for himself by coming up with an idea he thought was so big that it would make him a legitimate, credible inventor and an incredibly wealthy man: an air freshener system built directly into automobiles. He saw it as a solution for people who want to keep their cars smelling fresh but do not want to keep buying unattractive air fresheners. He also saw it as a valuable option car manufacturers could offer to consumers, giving them a market advantage.

Nothing like it was on the market, and he thought it was a truly original idea, like his other inspired ideas. So he jumped right in.

William paid for product designs, blueprints, and prototypes. He spent hours researching costs and making sales presentations to potential buyers and investors.

But William also had his hand in several other ventures that he thought might also pan out.

That was his problem. He was working a full-time job while pursuing multiple invention schemes, spreading himself too thin to put all of his attention into any single idea or project.

The end result was far from successful. He spent thousands of dollars and countless hours before discovering that years before someone had invented the exact same system. As quickly as his journey began, it came to an abrupt halt.

Because William did not focus on one idea at a time, he overlooked a simple patent search, something that experienced inventors know to do before investing any time or money in a project.

WHAT NOT TO DO:

❐ Aim at more than one target at a time.

ADVICE:

❐ Focus on one opportunity at a time.
❐ Learn to fail on paper before failing for real.
 Examine and research an idea before you invest time
 and money into it.

If it turns out that an opportunity is not worth the risk, time, or effort, regroup and keep searching for the ones that will bring you closer to your lifelong goals.

BRING LIFE INTO FOCUS

If you discover an opportunity that fits into your lifetime achievement plans, it's time to get focused. Prioritize your goals by weighing the consequences, thinking of the time limitations, and comparing the pros and cons.

Realize your purpose. When you start working toward your lifelong aspirations, you quickly build momentum. The usual distractions that drain your energy will still be there, but you will have a purpose to keep you motivated and focused. This makes it easier to ignore or push aside those pesky daily distractions.

STAY FOCUSED

To stay focused on a new opportunity, clarify your short-term objectives by revisiting your list of goals and daily tasks. Avoid distractions by finding a quiet place to concentrate, and set aside a fixed amount of time each day to work on prioritizing your goals and tasks.

Master your skills, analyze advice, conduct research, work hard, and train your mental focus like a laser beam on a target to improve your chances of success. Let go of self-imposed expectations about how society thinks you should live your life. Pursue what makes you happy and that will likely be one of the best contributions you can possibly make to yourself, your family, your community, and the world at large.

These are simple principles when taken by themselves. Taken together they can sometimes be difficult to keep track of and manage. But if you stay focused, you can do it. You will be rewarded with a fuller, more satisfying pursuit of your opportunity, which will yield positive, sustainable results.

Don't forget that to stay focused, try to eliminate as many distractions as possible, because life's distractions not only steal your focus, but also drain your energy. That's why professional boxers often prepare for championships at isolated training camps, away from energy-sapping influences and mind-boggling distractions.

Complete the incompletes in your life. The more unfinished projects and tasks you have, the thinner your energy and attention will be spread. If you have a tendency to start projects and not complete them, stop jumping from one to the other and focus on one at a time. These tasks can range from items around your home that need to be fixed to intriguing business ideas you scribbled on a piece of paper.

Experts say that your attention can be focused on only a certain number of projects at once. Most agree that six is the maximum, and even that number can dilute your concentration. When your focus is spread beyond what you can handle, you will feel less motivated to pursue any of your goals.

If you cannot tie up your unfinished business, scratch those incompletes off your to-do list. Focus on what's important and take advantage of rare opportunities that have the potential to improve your entire life.

AVOID LIFE'S DISTRACTIONS

Life has a way of putting obstacles in our way at the most inopportune times. Most are distractions, ranging from something as simple as a ringing phone to a nagging thought that consumes your mind. Some distractions are easy enough to ignore; others are a bit more challenging. But if we're not careful, these distractions can gobble up great opportunities as we fail to do the critical things necessary to achieve our goals.

Create Positive Daily Rituals

Review your long-term goals frequently. Revisit your short-term goals each and every day. This will keep your subconscious mind engaged and focused on your lifelong objectives as you consistently and consciously work toward your immediate goals.

Prioritize Often

Weigh the consequences, think of the time limitations, compare the positives and negatives, and then weed out the junk. Keep rearranging your goals as circumstances change and unexpected opportunities present themselves to ensure that the most important priorities always rise to the top of your action list.

Know Yourself

When you know yourself you become aware of your strengths, and, more important, you learn to identify the weaknesses that can get in the way of success. Then you can objectively look at issues and obstacles that crop up to find a solution. For example, rather than getting discouraged that there isn't enough time in your day, keep a healthy perspective. Be honest to acknowledge that limitation. Then you will be able to figure out what is distracting you and how you want to respond.

Improve Mental Focus

Use techniques like meditation or deep concentration to help you get into the flow or zone and clarify your mental focus. Practice these daily, just as you would any kind of physical exercise, and your ability to concentrate and laser in on your current task will increase significantly.

Create a Work Sanctuary

Our environment or surroundings can either distract or help us focus, so intentionally carve out a space for yourself that insulates you from distractions so you can perform your best work. If you work best in absolute quiet, eliminate background noise. Don't have the television on while trying to work. If you need white noise to get you into the zone, play soothing music. Minimize intrusions like people interrupting you or phones beeping.

Recharge Your Batteries

Tiredness and fatigue can be the worst kind of distraction, so get enough sleep, eat right, and exercise regularly to avoid feeling sluggish or ill. Keeping yourself healthy will improve all of your mental faculties and will also help you deal with stress without letting it slow you down or impair your judgment.

Don't Procrastinate

Remember that procrastination is the thief of time. Avoid delaying any of your tasks—even the small ones—by leaving them for tomorrow, next week, or next month. Do it now, feel that great immediate sense of accomplishment, and then move on to the next project and the next higher rung in your ladder to success.

Empower Yourself

Develop your willpower and complete everything you start. Willfully stop straying thoughts and bring them back to the task at hand. When you feel the urge to give up, push through it and go an extra mile to prove to yourself that you can meet adversity without wavering. You will build positive work habits, improve your confidence and determination, and ensure that you don't get scattered and spread too thin.

Don't Multitask

Focus on one thing at a time. Remember, Ready . . . Aim . . . Fire! Back in the 1990s, people used to pride themselves on being able to multitask. But now research shows that those who multitask are less effective and have less cognitive ability than people who do one thing with full attention before moving to the next task.

Ask for Help

Communicate with others about what your goals are. Ask friends and family members for help. If you can ask for help to reduce your workload, you can spend more time focusing on your goals. People like to pitch in and lend a hand because it makes them feel good about themselves, so don't be shy about asking for what you need.

Learn to Say No

Don't take on unnecessary responsibilities. Be there for the people who need you, but remember that to help others you first have to be there for yourself and what you need in life. If people ask you to do something for them, be honest. If you are working on a project and don't want to lose your concentration, offer to help another time or opt out completely.

Give It a Break

Taking breaks will help you maintain focus and refresh your mind. You can work continuously for forty-eight minutes, followed by a twelve-minute break, or use whatever ratio you feel works best for you. The important thing is to take small breaks during your workday. Taking breaks like this is not slacking off; it just means you are keeping yourself in top performance mode to accomplish more.

There will always be distractions you cannot get rid of, but by avoiding those you can at least control, you will immensely increase your productivity and will stay more motivated to work toward your primary objectives.

You can always find a distraction if you're looking for one.

Tom Kite

Observe the Masses and Do the Opposite

– 6 –

Far too many people think their daily routines are just more of the same, day in, day out. They are like hamsters slaving away mindlessly on a treadmill to nowhere. If you sometimes view your own life in the same way, we wrote this chapter specifically for you. The lessons you'll learn will change your perspective by showing you how to break negative habits, stop following the herd, and start achieving your own unique goals so that every day is a fresh, exciting, positive step in the right direction.

Most of our lives are routine and may seem mundane. Most of us define our typical schedules as the "daily grind." You get up, perform your morning rituals, take care of the kids, head off to work, come home, do chores, make dinner, and collapse on the couch in front of the TV. After a while you stumble off to bed, and when the alarm goes off a few hours later, you grudgingly do it all over again. No wonder life seems to pass us by in a flash, leaving us feeling vacant and bored. If you are living in a vicious cycle that never seems to have a beginning or end and you don't find time to discover the opportunities around you, you will never reach your lifelong dreams and goals.

Some people have a gloomy outlook, not wanting to get up in the morning, dreading work, or feeling dissatisfied with their home lives. They may hate their jobs, resent their bosses or coworkers, or prefer to stay away from home because of tension caused by unhealthy relationships with family members. They spend the weekends lounging around, pretending to relax, but, truth be told, they have knots in their stomachs because Monday is fast approaching.

Have you ever had a job that gave you that sinking feeling in your stomach every Sunday night? Does it seem you can never catch a break? Do you feel as though life just drags on and each day is a continuation of the previous one? Those sentiments are not uncommon in today's society, but understand that happiness or sadness and your perception of the passage of time all stem from your individually constructed perspective on life.

If you view life as a struggle, you'll interpret everything that happens to you in that light. You'll live your life in a way that validates and confirms your point of view, and it will always feel like an intense uphill climb. But a change to an optimistic outlook will generate more positive actions and a fresher routine, which is how you begin to create a new you.

Keep in mind that it is your prerogative not to change. You can stay on the treadmill forever. Just don't complain about your life not being where you want it to be. If you aren't willing to make the effort to grab hold of your goals, nobody will want to listen to you whine.

Is your ultimate goal just to survive the grind and get through each day in one piece? Or do you believe that life is yours to do with as you choose, being the architect of your own destiny? Some architects think small and are lazy, so they construct doublewides that look like every other trailer home in the park. Then there are those who shoot for the Taj Mahal. If they don't make it, they still wind up with a unique and wonderful place they are proud to call their own.

So don't sell yourself short. Don't stay stuck in the rut of daily habits and routines, letting opportunities fly past unnoticed. March to the beat of a different drummer. Instead of lagging behind with tired feet and blisters, you might wind up sprinting across the goal line—or at least dancing to your heart's content.

Habit and routine have an unbelievable power to waste and destroy.

Henri de Lubac

INSTITUTIONALIZED

The term institutionalization describes the process by which inmates are shaped and transformed by the standardized environments in which they live. When inmates become institutionalized—they stop questioning the way things are done and go with the flow. Institutionalization involves the incorporation of the routines of life into one's habits of thinking, feeling, and acting. Sociologists, psychologists, and psychiatrists have studied this process extensively.

While I was working for the Drug Enforcement Administration, I was placed in an international drug and money laundering Strike Force. The group included an FBI agent, two NYPD detectives, an IRS agent, and two other DEA agents. Because I was fresh out of the academy, the other DEA agents—well–respected, seasoned veterans—were appointed to be my mentors.

At first I couldn't tell if they loved or hated what they did. Both seemed unfazed by the crazy schedule of being called to duty at all times of the day or night. But we worked long hours, and my mentors complained the entire time. They complained about everything, and the job was just one item on a long list of chronic gripes. After working with them for a few years, I saw the two as very smart and hardworking agents but completely miserable guys.

Whenever I voiced suggestions or criticisms of how something was done, they said, "Don't worry, you'll learn to live with it. You'll become institutionalized just like us."

"What do you mean 'institutionalized'?"

"When you spend enough time here, you learn to accept everything and not question the institution."

They went on to explain that when you work for an organization long enough, you become complacent and get used to the routine, even in a rather interesting position as a DEA special agent, which is far removed from the daily routines most people experience.

"Don't question the institution" became a daily mantra with them . . . and me. It was funny at first, their expressions and the emphatic way they'd wave their hands as they said "institutionalized."

But then one day it truly sank in; they were right! From that moment on I went to work and tried to imagine the future and what I was going to become over the next fifteen years. What I saw was a cynical, unhappy agent with a backbreaking schedule who never questioned the status quo. "That's just how it's done," I'd tell myself, as I continued just to exist in a world that felt like one great big hamster wheel populated with other complacent ratracers.

The more I contemplated my situation, the more I began to recognize that I wasn't happy with the direction my life was going, and I was not the kind of person who responded well to being institutionalized. As the Chinese proverb says, "If you don't change the direction you're headed, you will wind up where you are going." So when an opportunity came knocking, I answered immediately and left my career as a DEA special agent. Ever since, I have thanked those guys for opening my eyes so that I could wake up from that comfortably numb routine and passionately pursue my dreams of success.

The same institutionalization process occurs outside the prison walls to a great number of the population. Many people become drones enslaved by their routines and unconscious habits and patterns. But the process is not limited to a particular worksite environment or social structure because institutionalization is a mind-set. You could be a traveling salesperson, housewife, college student, public servant, or an entrepreneur who works at home. But if you are just repeating your routine over and over again, without questions, healthy curiosity, imagination, or positive emotions, you are running the risk of becoming institutionalized.

Like all processes of gradual change, this one typically occurs in stages, and the longer one remains stuck in the same routine, the more significant and deeply rooted their institutionalization will be. Those who have become conditioned like this over a long period of time start to think less about the outside world and concentrate only on what is right in front of them in their immediate surroundings. They see fewer options, alternatives, and opportunities because tunnel vision limits their outlook. And you cannot take advantage of opportunities if you don't recognize them.

People gradually become so accustomed to their environments, whether it's a tiny office cubicle, a classroom, or the den at home, they forget their greater dreams, visions, and lifelong goals. They put their noses to the grindstone and look straight ahead, trudging from one weekend to the next, from one paycheck to the next paycheck. They never reveal their inner desires to anyone, and eventually they lose sight of them altogether, becoming like a donkey focused only on a carrot dangling at the end of a stick.

Why do so many people get stuck in the same routine for twenty, thirty, or forty years? Most people just don't think about it. We are conditioned to accept life as it is, with no questions asked. We are raised to get a job, hopefully a stable one, and do what is expected of us without bucking the system. Day after day we get up, go to work, come home, go to sleep, and then start the whole process over again. We were told to do this by our parents, our teachers, our television sets, and the collective society. The process of institutionalization is subtle and most people don't realize it's happening to them. They don't consciously choose to give in and give up, surrendering to a cookie-cutter life. It just happens; the way a kid grows taller without noticing it until one day he looks in the mirror and sees that he's six foot four.

Because people aren't aware that it is happening to them, they become ever more mired and dependent until following these dead-end paths and routines becomes automatic and second nature. When they see other people stepping out on their own, they think it's slightly weird, risky, and unconventional. Ask them for career advice and they'll tell you to stick to the middle road and don't make waves.

There are so many sad, heartbreaking stories of people who had worked for many years at the same company only to get laid off for one reason or another. They had put the majority of their waking hours into their jobs, which had become their daily routines and a huge part of their self-image. Some people even go as far as committing suicide because they feel that without their work routines, they are less of a person and their lives are fruitless and useless. This is how powerful a routine can become. Sometimes choosing the right routine, the one that helps you feel good about yourself and realize your dreams, can be a matter of life and death.

Many people don't give a thought to their daily routines; they just move through them in a haze. Don't sleepwalk through life. Ask questions or give suggestions. Don't become institutionalized. Don't lose sight of your long-term objectives. Assert yourself and your willpower. If you become institutionalized, you won't ever be able to recognize opportunities when they arise, let alone take advantage of them.

MISSED OP:
Special Agent to Super Mario

I couldn't believe it. I read through the letter again.

I was accepted into the basic agent training academy for the Drug Enforcement Administration. Not exactly a James Bond type of thing but it had its share of excitement and perks. It certainly had provided a comfortable lifestyle for myself and my family. My wife Marcie and I and our three children, Daniel, Mary and little Ben had a nice home and could afford all the basic necessities.

But there had always been that other dream, the one most people envision at some time or another, the dream of being financially independent while working in a field I was passionate about.

As a child I had loved playing video games and computer games. I'd dreamed of inventing wonderful games, the best in the world. As an adult, this dream had given way to working with the DEA and had become a hobby.

I'd developed some games I was pretty proud of. I enjoyed playing them, as did my children. I'd come up with one I was especially proud of. I'd put together a proposal and sent it off to some companies, not really expecting much to come of it.

But now here it was, the chance of a lifetime some would call it. The door of my childhood dream opening wide and all I had to do was step through it.

"Well, you look pretty pleased over something," Marcie said as she stepped into the room. "Don't tell me you won the sweepstakes." She was only half joking. She knows me like a book and she knew I was thrilled over something.

"Here, read this," I told her, handing her the letter I'd been reading over and over.

"Oh, Phil," she breathed after reading the letter. "The chance to be on the lead design team of your own game. This is your dream of a lifetime, isn't it? I say let's go for it. If you don't, you'll always wonder what if. Whatever you decide to do is absolutely right with me. I'm so proud of you, getting an offer like this, but then, I've always been proud of you in all that you've done, you know that." She leaned against me and hugged me as she handed back my dream letter.

"Whatever we decide, I'm going to get a frame and hang this right up on the wall where we can see it every day," I told her.

"I'll go out and buy you a frame this very afternoon."

"It would mean giving up our home here and moving to California. Giving up my job, leaving friends, the kids starting over in new schools. Leaving our families."

"There are planes," she reminded me. "We could visit and telephone and there's always e-mail. Besides, wherever you are is my home."

"Thank you for that. But I want you to think about it. My job with the DEA is a pretty secure one. This, as wonderful as it sounds and as big as the computer industry is, is still a pie-in-the-sky sort of thing. We could give up everything to enter into this and it could be wonderful. It could make our dreams come true as well as give us the opportunity to help friends and family make their dreams come true. Oh, Marcie, if it works out we could do so much!

But if it doesn't work out, we could lose so much, too.

In that instant I decided that it just wasn't realistic. I couldn't leave my job that I had worked so hard for and risk my family's future all for a chance to follow a pipe dream. Besides, many people would kill for the life I already had. My friends and family said I had everything; a good job, a house and a family who loved me.

Now, looking back on a basically satisfying career, I still have a burning regret of not taking that chance. I still look at that letter and ask myself, "What if?"

Deep down in my heart I can almost see what I would have become. I know that I could have made that work. I read the success stories of others and what they accomplished and think what people might have said to them when they risked all they had to follow a dream.

If they could be innovators, why can't I? It takes a lot of courage to risk what others perceive as having everything on a dream that might yield nothing.

WHAT NOT TO DO:

❏ Conform to the norm because it is what everyone expects of you.

ADVICE:

❏ Don't avoid risks because you are comfortable where you are.

❏ Weigh taking a chance versus the regret of not taking a chance. Can you live with the outcome of either?

LOSING TRACK OF TIME

Why did time seem to move so much slower when we were children? I can remember summers that lasted forever, and now it is hard to keep track of years and decades. As people get older the passage of time seems to accelerate, and no one is exactly sure why this perception, or misperception, occurs.

Some scientists theorize that when you experience something for the very first time, you expend more energy on it and therefore recall details of the event more clearly. That information is stored in the memory in a new way instead of mingling it with previous experiences. Think of the first time you did anything significant in your life: your first kiss, your first day of school, your first job, or your first time behind the wheel of a car. You will have more vivid memories of any kinds of things you invested lots of energy into than you will of the things you've done many times.

Later in life, repetition and routine begins to make our memories seem vague or fuzzy. The habit of doing the same thing frequently makes time feel as if it is flying by. Time wasn't really moving slower in the past than it is in the present. It just feels that way because we've fallen into habitual patterns and routines that are not as new, fresh, and exciting.

A habit is best defined as a recurrent, often unconscious, pattern of behavior that is acquired through frequent repetition. And a routine is a procedure or set of activities that occur on a regular, continual basis or schedule.

Most of life is both habitual and routine. Routines and habits facilitate repeated behaviors to enable us to organize our lives to do the same things we did yesterday, the day before, the week before, and the month before. They can go on for years and years. It's estimated that out of every 11,000 signals we receive from our senses, the brain consciously processes only forty.

Our routines and habits condition us to disregard a lot of sensory information we receive, which can sometimes make us more efficient. We use routines and habits to remember how to find the car keys, drive the car, pick up the kids from school on time, and find home without a map. That's all well and good, and some routines and habits, like brushing teeth or going to the gym, are useful. But if you go through life as if the whole process of living is one unconscious routine, you'll waste valuable time because you'll become complacent and lose track of many precious minutes, hours, days, weeks, months, and years.

Routines and habits are powerful enough to put us into a semiconscious state of mind while we perform everyday tasks. How many times have you returned from a long commute and realized that you could not even remember the drive home because your mind was on autopilot? You sit in front of the television and before you know it, hours have elapsed. Your wife speaks to you but you've zoned out and don't hear a thing. You stand on the scale and wonder how you gained all that weight without noticing it. You look through your scrapbook and ask yourself, "Where did the time go?" The answer is that you have been hypnotized by your daily routines.

In addition to squandering a great amount of time, being complacent also means we cannot take advantage of opportunities because we do not see them. When we don't take notice of the little things around us, we miss out on the vast number of opportunities that are out there all the time. Remember that big opportunities can stem from small problems or circumstances. If you are just going through your routines and habits but failing to recognize all the potential that is around you, you are missing out on opportunities that can take you where you want to be.

As long as habit and routine dictate the pattern of living,
new dimensions of the soul will not emerge.

Henry Van Dyke

LEARN TO LIVE BY LIVING TO LEARN

Working at a new job is fresh and exciting because it's challenging. Meeting new people or experiencing different cultures is definitely interesting to most of us, but why? It is about the newness of those experiences. What makes it new to us is the feeling of learning something we didn't know before that demands our attention! For example, the first time you drove a car, the experience was all about learning. You were thrilled and focused, whereas now that you are an accomplished driver and believe that there is nothing new to learn, you can drive all the way to work while in a trance. Meeting new people, doing new things, and taking on fresh challenges is all about learning. Learning is the key to staying aware and excited about life. Become a lifetime learner and you'll live a more complete life.

If our habits and routines are not propelling us closer to our goals and dreams, we must change them. We have to infuse learning into our daily lives. Knowing how to incorporate learning into your routines will fill you with enthusiasm, renewed interest, and sustainable motivation. Getting into the habit of learning new things and making learning part of every routine will feel like time is expanding instead of fleeting, which will not only prepare you for various difficult situations or obstacles in life, but also uncover opportunities that are lying in wait. Life will regain its interest and mystery, and lots of hidden gems will be revealed to you that you would otherwise sleepwalk right past without seeing.

CHANGE YOUR HABITS AND ROUTINES

Habits and routines, good or bad, make you who you are. The key is controlling them or changing them so that they serve you instead of the other way around. If you know how to eliminate bad habits and create positive ones, then even the smallest effort can create big results.

The key is to cut down on habits and routines that are not taking you where you want to go and replace them with the routines and habits that will help you achieve what you want. If you think that is easier said than done, you are right, because it will take a lot of hard work and perseverance to accomplish your transformation. But it can be done. The more you learn to change bad habits, the easier it becomes. And the rewards are priceless.

Humans are creatures of habit and routine. As we grow up we develop behaviors that stay with us for a lifetime. Those behaviors turn into routines, and those routines become habits in our adult lives. Some of those behaviors may not be healthy or helpful in getting us where we want to be. But we can consciously and subconsciously change the non-progressive habits and transform them into progressive ones.

Change won't happen overnight. If something takes years to learn, it will require a significant amount of work to undo. But the simplest routines to change are the smallest ones and "inch by inch it's a cinch." For some people that first step will be to take a daily vitamin or commit to exercising a couple of times a week. For others it might mean reading at least four books a month or completing a weekly project around the house.

Before you start removing old routines, though, first try to add some new positive ones. That way support will be in place so that when you drop an old habit, you won't have a void feeling or empty space in your life. The real key to changing habits and routines is to eventually swap out existing negative or useless ones for new positive ones. This way you prepare yourself to jump on opportunities that may arise by creating an environment that is positive and advantageous. Also, you'll be able to discover additional opportunities while performing your new routines. Start taking positive action toward your lifetime goals, inch by inch and then step by step.

TWENTY-ONE-DAY PLAN

Experts and professional trainers provide plenty of evidence that if we focus and condition ourselves to do something for twenty-one days in a row, that action becomes ingrained as a habit and part of our routines. The point of a habit is that it doesn't require thought; it is automatic. So perform the action as correctly and consistently as possible and repeat it every day for twenty-one days, preferably at the same time each day. This will ensure that the new habit is drilled into your subconscious mind.

ADD POSITIVE ROUTINES

WRITE IT DOWN

Write commitments on paper. If you add a new activity to your routine, write down what it is, what it will help you achieve, and what time of day you will perform it. This will enhance clarity by defining the specifics and will also create accountability. Writing it down also helps imprint the activity onto your conscious and subconscious mind as something you must do.

BE ACCOUNTABLE TO SOMEONE

If you want to add a positive behavior or remove a negative one, find a supportive friend, peer, or family member to be your teammate in the effort. When you go into something with a buddy or partner, you feel accountable to them not to fail, so you try harder than if you were going it alone. Your accountability partner(s) will also give you moral support, so try to enlist people who have a positive, can-do attitude. You don't want a quitter or slacker for a buddy. Tell other people about your new habit. Even if they just ask you once in a while how it's going, that reinforces your drive to accomplish your goal. Try giving someone money or some other object you value to hold for you, on the condition that they return it only when you've successfully completed your new twenty-one-consecutive days routine.

RemoveNegative Routines

Bad habits are like a comfortable bed,
easy to get into, but hard to get out of.

Proverb

BEHAVIORAL TRIGGERS

A behavioral trigger is a short ritual or act performed before doing a bad habit. Try wearing a rubber band around your wrist, and every time you have the urge to perform that bad habit, snap the rubber band and ask yourself, "How will this help me become successful?" The trigger reminds you to stay focused on what is healthy and positive. Consistently using a trigger helps condition the mind to a new pattern of behavior because it is a kinesthetic or bodily action-based reminder.

REPLACE BAD HABITS WITH GOOD HABITS

Yanking bad habits without replacing or satisfying the urges and needs they fulfill is a sure way not to succeed. This is why so many smokers gain weight after they give up smoking. Nicotine suppresses appetite slightly but ex-smokers gain the majority of their weight because they replace bad smoking habits with bad eating habits. So if you want to give up, say, television, find a new way to relax, such as reading, listening to audiobooks, learning the banjo, playing chess, going for a hike, or meditating.

FOCUS ON ONE HABIT

Focus on only one area of change at a time. Remember that aiming at more than one target will result in not hitting any of them.

ROUTINES OF SUCCESSFUL PEOPLE

Jim Citrin from Yahoo! Finance did a study on the daily routines of twenty successful CEOs. In his study he found an overwhelming similarity between the daily routines of all twenty. The three most significant similarities were (1) starting the day early, (2) exercising regularly, and (3) spending time with their families. [10]

The early bird gets the worm! All the CEOs started early and said it was because that is the part of their daily routines over which they have the greatest amount of control. The latest that any of these executives get up is 6:00am, and about 80 percent of them rise by 5:30 or earlier. To fit the most into each day, start early.

The second commonality was exercise. Many of the most successful people in the world exercise regularly. More than 70 percent of the CEOs surveyed exercise in the morning, while 15 percent do it during the day. Only two of the executives admitted to not exercising on a regular basis.

Spending quality time with family was the other important part of their daily routines. They find that mornings seem to work best for encouraging significant family time, and family interaction is a central part of their daily life.

President Barack Obama follows a schedule and routine that is similar to those of the twenty CEOs in the study. He likes to have his workout with weights and cardio training first thing in the morning, at 6:45. He reads several papers, eats breakfast with his family, and helps pack his daughters off to school before starting his workday. By 9:00 he's in the Oval Office. In the evening he eats dinner with his family and then often returns to work. He can be seen working many nights until 10 pm. Regardless of whether or not you agree with his politics, Barack Obama is a highly successful individual who leverages positive habits and healthy routines to achieve everything he wants out of life, and we can all learn from his example.

Overall, successful people have good habits and follow positive routines.

Embrace Opportunity

A successful person grasps each opportunity and examines it closely to see if it can bring them closer to their lifetime goals and dreams. When you encounter a situation, make it a habit to ask yourself, "Is this my opportunity?" and "How can this help me advance toward my goals?" No matter how busy your routine may be, it is imperative that you pause to ask those questions on a daily basis as one of your progressive habits.

POSITIVE ROUTINES AND HABITS

Not sure what beneficial routines and habits will help you on your way to success? Incorporate some or all of these positive resources into your life.

Audiobooks

Thousands of educational and motivational audiobooks are on the market today. Listen to these throughout the day to learn something that will get you closer to your lifelong goals. Listen to audiobooks while doing many other tasks, including commuting to work, exercising, shopping, cooking, showering, working outdoors, or any other solitary activity. Make listening to positive audiobooks a daily habit. If you listen to just thirty minutes of an audiobook a day, that gives you 182 hours of extra learning and motivation per year. That is the equivalent of a full-time college semester!

Self-Improvement or Motivational Seminars

Many expert self-improvement and motivational speakers provide workshops and seminars that assist you in uncovering your talents and creating new opportunities. Jack Canfield and Tony Robbins are two of the most acclaimed, and if you have a chance, I urge you to attend one of their events. Not only will their seminars help you reach your goals, but many of the attendees will share the same interests as you. Seminars are a great place to network and open doors to additional opportunities. Make going to a positive seminar part of your monthly or yearly routine.

Mentors and Coaches

Make speaking or collaborating with a mentor part of your routine. You can find a mentor online, or use someone you work with or know through your social network. Ask that person out to lunch, tell him that you admire what he has accomplished. Or ask her if you can pick her brain about how she achieved her goal. Get permission to call or e-mail from time to time to ask for advice. Make it part of your weekly, biweekly, or monthly routine.

Groups and Organizations

Join or create a group of like-minded people. Mastermind and brain-storming groups are listed all over the Internet, and meeting with these groups on a biweekly basis will do several positive things. First, groups will provide a support network to keep you motivated and accountable for doing what you say you're going to do. Second, if you have a problem or lose focus, you have a support network to talk to about it and to help you find solutions. Last, meeting and discussing ideas with people will open new doors of opportunity and create lasting bonds and networks you may need in the future.

Diet and Nutrition

A healthy diet should be part of everyone's daily routine. Following a healthy diet will give you energy and keep you going for longer periods of time, while protecting you from sickness and disease. Eating right ensures that your brain is nourished and your mind is fresh and alert.

Physical Exercise

Another habit everyone should develop is regular physical exercise. Following an exercise program can be difficult to start, but once you get it underway, it will be even harder to quit because exercise makes you feel better and look your best. The benefits are numerous and include a generally healthier body and stronger immune system, increased strength and endurance, less stress, and a better night's sleep followed by more sustainable energy all day long. As your physique becomes toned, so does your mind, and having the discipline and confidence to embark on a steady exercise regimen can give you a mental edge that puts you at the top of your game and rewards you with enhanced self-esteem, clarity, and focus.

Staying healthy is priceless and should be at the top of the list of whatever other skills you learn. You cannot take advantage of an opportunity if you are sick; if you drop dead, you won't be able to apply any of the knowledge and wisdom you spent so much time learning.

Motivation is what gets you started. Habit is what keeps you going.

Jim Ryun

STAND APART FROM THE CROWD

In today's competitive world, the difference between success and failure can be a thin margin, and the advantage often comes down to you and what you have that the competition lacks. So how can you make yourself more attractive to the world to ensure that winning edge? Become more marketable by acquiring new and diverse skills that separate you from the crowd and give you the value-added distinction that sets you apart from your competitors.

Picture yourself sitting in a large waiting room. You will be pitching an idea for an import-export business to a well-known and successful venture capitalist. Sitting next to you is another person whose meeting with the same decision maker is scheduled right after yours. You both have the same objective. You both have been presented with a huge opportunity to get the money you need to start your business.

All other things being equal, you can speak English, Spanish, and Chinese, and recently competed in a triathlon where you finished in the top ten out of a field of more than 100 athletes. You have a written business plan prepared with the help of a mentor, you have a professional website, and you are involved with several networking organizations. You get up with the sun every morning and make a to-do list based on both short- and long-term goals. You're reading a motivational book about personal finance while you wait.

The person sitting next to you speaks only one language and has done nothing to promote his business other than write his proposal. He's tired and looks it because he just ate a huge meal of junk food. He is thumbing through a two-seasons-old Sports Illustrated he found on the table in the waiting room.

Before you both walk into the conference room, ask yourself, "Who has the advantage? Who is outstanding?" It may be true that the other person has a better proposal, but it could be your additional traits that make you stand out from the crowd in a positive way.

Make learning new skills part of your routine. As mentioned before, you can listen to audiobooks to learn new languages, business subjects, public speaking skills, finance, history, computer science, psychology, law, or any other topic imaginable. Take classes on weeknights, weekends, or online. Join clubs, organizations, or local colleges that teach skills you're interested in acquiring.

Here is a list of possible skills and activities that might give you an advantage when presented with a new opportunity:

❐ Acquire computer software, typing, website design, social networking, and e-commerce skills
❐ Learn a second or third language or the rules of business etiquette and protocol in a multicultural global world
❐ Study martial arts, pistol and rifle marksmanship, or verbal judo
❐ Train in first aid and get CPR and AED certifications
❐ Learn to jog, train for a marathon, practice yoga, or become a weight lifter
❐ Master photography, musicianship, writing, or public speaking
❐ Get a real estate license or mortgage broker certification
❐ Take classes on how to paint or sculpt, or how to make pottery or jewelry

❒ Coach a sports team, join a team, or learn to play golf

❒ Learn bartending or professional catering

❒ Develop team-building skills, do a project adventure course, or enroll in Six Sigma business training.

❒ Learn mountain climbing, skiing, cycling, or wilderness survival.

❒ Become certified as a personal trainer, yoga teacher, or aerobics instructor.

❒ Get trained as a massage, aromatherapy, or acupuncture therapist.

❒ Train for your pilot's license, boating license, commercial trucker's license, or teaching certificate.

The list is as long as your imagination. Whatever your daily routine is, start adding additional skills to your repertoire. Even if you cannot see any opportunities in your immediate future, start separating yourself from the crowd now. Adding additional skills will not only prepare you for new opportunities and open new doors of opportunity but will also move you ahead of others to give you a competitive edge and head start when opportunities appear.

All of the top achievers I know are life-long learners . . . Looking for new skills, insights, and ideas. If they're not learning, they're not growing . . . not moving toward excellence.

Denis Waitley

Why Not You?

- 7 -

If something great is going to happen somewhere in the world, why can't it happen to you? You can accomplish anything you want if you will just realize that it is possible and that it is yours to go out and get.

Whenever an opportunity reveals itself, someone is going to take advantage of it. Whether that person is you or someone else depends on your actions, how quickly you gain the knowledge to exploit the opportunity, how focused and prepared you are, how much effort you put into achieving it, and how much you believe you can and will do it.

If you prepared yourself by understanding and applying yourself to the process to take full advantage of an opportunity, then belief in yourself comes naturally. That confidence comes from your personal experience and that of others who missed opportunities before you. Create or develop your internal motivation to keep you moving in the right direction, like a built-in mental and emotional compass pointed toward ultimate success. When you have cultivated the tools needed to achieve whatever you want, it is easy to visualize yourself already in the winner's circle.

If you don't achieve what you dream, who will? Make your mind-set that you can be the one! Throughout history people have been told they can't do this or that because of whatever reasons. But every single accomplishment has a person behind it and there is no reason why you cannot be a member of that club. You want to become a billionaire? Why not? You want to break a world record? Go for it. You want to win a Noble Prize? Start working toward it. Remember, if you don't take advantage of your opportunities, someone else will.

Christopher Columbus, Orville and Wilbur Wright, Howard Hughes, Rosa Parks, and Albert Einstein were all told they couldn't do what they wanted, or they were accused of being crazy. The girlfriend of one of the young fellows who invented YouTube broke up with him a few months before he became a billionaire, because she thought he should abandon his silly YouTube dream and get a real job.

All of these extraordinary people went on to do great things and prove others wrong. They were the first in their fields to do what they set out to do, and they took advantage of their opportunities to become international icons by doing what people said they shouldn't, couldn't, and wouldn't.

MISSED OP:
Never Good Enough

In the first grade, I wanted to try out for a solo singing part in our Christmas program, but when I found out that Megan Wolfard, the best singer in the entire first grade, was also auditioning for the same role, I chickened out.

In the sixth grade, I wanted to try out for the middle school cheerleading squad. I had always enjoyed gymnastics, and I felt it was something I was genuinely good at. I showed up to auditions, and after watching thirteen skinny, agile, natural-born gymnasts perform flawless back handsprings and mid-air toe touches with ease, I turned around and ran the other direction before anyone saw that I was there.

In my senior year in high school, I wanted to ask Brandon Kistler, whom I had adored since my sixth grade not-cheerleading days, to the prom. I came close a few times, but never close enough. I was fifteen pounds overweight, had really bad hair, or so I thought, and Brandon deserved better. In the end, Megan Wolfard asked him to prom and they made a beautiful couple. I stayed home and watched Lifetime Movie Network.

I think by now, you have a pretty good idea of what my problem has been all my life. Every time I feel I'm good at something or in any way adequate, it always seems someone who is better inadvertently puts me back in my place. Maybe it's a psychological problem; in fact,

I'm quite certain that it is, but when I feel someone is better than me at something I like to do, suddenly my own abilities seem invalidated. If I feel they are better than me, I stop believing I am good at that thing at all. I jump to the opposite extreme, and then I stop trying. In the first grade, all this cost me was a five-minute singing role. At twenty-seven, this cost me the life I had always wanted for myself.

❏ ❏ ❏

"The time has finally come that we are on the verge of releasing this new line of products," Edwin Fitch said, CEO of Buckle & Bruit's, a fast-growing baby toy company where I had managed to work myself about three-fourths of the way to the top. Right out of college I started out as a secretary for the company. Fitch got wind of my advertising ideas, which impressed him, and I was promoted, putting my marketing degree to use. After that, it was basically a domino effect. One successful advertising campaign after another, and I worked my way up the metaphorical staircase. Recently, the company's senior vice president decided (surprise, surprise), that motherhood was calling her name and she wasn't coming back from maternity leave. From that point on, her vacated job burned on my brain. The idea of being a successful executive for a nation-wide company kept me up at night. A position such as that one would bring me the kind of fulfillment for which I always hoped. And it wasn't even about the six figures, either.

Okay, I won't lie; the idea of six figures was exceptionally appealing.

"First things first," Fitch continued, despite my half-attentiveness. "Before we can launch this new product, we need to get the public excited about it!" Fitch slammed his fist down onto the desk, for emphasis I suppose, and then strolled to the other side of the long meeting table. "We need to produce an advertising campaign so enticing that every mother and father is camped outside one of our retailers at midnight on opening day."

I started doodling on my notebook, fighting the urge to shake my head. Fitch was on another one of his dramatic, passionate speeches. This could last anywhere from twenty minutes until the end of the workday.

"In order to produce the most effective results, I'm going to need one of you to head this campaign. If multiple people volunteer, which I suspect there will be more than one person interested, then I will use my own discretion to decide who is best equipped to run this project." Fitch paced back to the front of the room and stood behind his podium. He made eye contact with each and every one of us before continuing.

"As you know, an upper-level position has been vacant for about a month now. If you are at all interested in moving up in this company, I would highly recommend volunteering for this project, as I plan to evaluate the leadership qualities I look for in a senior vice president. Are there any questions?" When nobody said a word, he dismissed us to our normal workday and left the room.

At this point, my heart was seriously palpitating, and it wasn't the three cups of coffee I had this morning, either. This is my chance, I thought to myself, as I gathered my notebook and headed back to my tiny office. I walked down the hallway toward the elevator, pushed the down button, boarded the elevator, pushed the number for my floor, and rode the elevator ten stories down, operating off mental autopilot the entire time. I can do this, I know I can. I have made it this far in this company, based on my creative skills and my talent for marketing. This is something I like to do, this is something I'm good at, and becoming the senior vice president of this company is what I want! I could buy a nicer house, pay off my student loan, and take nice vacations, like drinking wine in Italy or eating sushi in Tokyo. But most important . . . I will have something to my name that will make me proud of myself. I. Can. Do. This.

My mind was made up, and I had never been so sure of anything. First thing the next morning, I would tell Fitch of my interest in leading the ad campaign for this new line of products. Confidence and determination would radiate from every one of my pores, and he would not doubt for a second who is the best person for the job. Tomorrow, I will—

"I am so excited about this new ad promotion! Do you think I should talk to Fitch about leading the campaign?"

I came to a hasty stop when I heard those words. I knew who the voice belonged to. I'd worked with Lillian Michaels for about three years, and she was amazing. She managed to come up with fantastic ideas that I would have never, in a million years, thought of myself. She is tactful and graceful and charming—the model of a perfect executive.

"I totally do think you should volunteer!" Lillian's friend responded. "Didn't you hear what he said? Basically, the person he chooses to head this campaign is the new senior vice president, and you would be perfect for that job! I think Fitch knows it too . . ."

I walked away before I heard any more. If Lillian was volunteering to lead the campaign, there was no way I would embarrass myself by attempting to be chosen over her. There would be absolutely no competition. This was completely stupid of me to even consider doing, I thought to myself as I got back into the elevator and headed for the first floor, fully intending to take the rest of the day off.

That night, I got very little sleep. I tossed and turned, threw the covers off and then wrapped back up in them. I got up four times to go to the bathroom, and twice for a glass of water. I thought about Megan Wolfard, who was a better singer than me in the first grade and a better prom date in the twelfth grade. An overwhelming bitterness overcome me, but, surprisingly, not toward Megan. I felt intense regret, and I knew that I had no one to blame but myself. Who was to say that Megan was better than me? I was the only one believing that, and I was the only one holding myself back. Who knows, maybe if I had more courage, I could have had the solo role in the first grade program and I could have danced the night away with Brandon Kistler!

"I'm not letting this happen to me again!" I shouted. "Megan Wolfard was not better than me, and neither is Lillian Michaels! This project belongs to me, and tomorrow I am taking what is mine!"

As soon as I came to this decision, I was finally able to fall asleep.

The next morning, the first place I went was to the office of Mr. Edwin Fitch. I was ready to volunteer, and I felt confident that I was the right person for the job. I already had my mini-speech planned out and had rehearsed it in front of the mirror for the first thirty minutes of my morning.

I paused before Fitch's office door. I straightened the bottom of my blouse and brushed my hands on the top of my pants. I raised my hand to knock on Fitch's office door. Before I was able to, however, the door swung open, and Lillian Michaels stood before me.

"Oh, hey, Christy I guess we are both hoping to lead this new ad campaign, huh? I just got through talking to Fitch about it myself."

My heart dropped to my toes, and just like that, all of my personal pep talks and rehearsing flew out the window. I literally stared my competition in the face, and I had never felt more inadequate or foolish for my ambitions. I forced a smile.

"Oh, no, I wasn't volunteering! I'm not interested in all that responsibility. I was just going to talk to him about when I can take my vacation week."

"Ah, I see," Lillian replied. "Well, I hope you get the week off that you need! Have a great day, Christy!"

As soon as she was out of sight, I hurried off in the other direction.

I called off the rest of that week. I told Fitch that I was sick, which was not entirely a lie. I was sick. I was sick of not feeling good enough, and I was sick that for my entire life I had given up before I ever tried. I was sick that every time I finally felt confident about a certain ability I had, someone always came along to make me feel inferior. And frankly, all this "feeling sick" had me literally feeling sick to my stomach, to the point I could justifiably say that I had the stomach flu.

On Friday, Fitch called to check up on how I was feeling. I told him I was better, and should be back in the office by Monday. Before hanging up, he said, "You know, Christy, I was really surprised when you did not volunteer to lead the ad campaign for the new product line. You do such wonderful work, and I really thought you would make a wonderful leader in this company."

My breath caught in my throat. "Oh, well, you know, I—"

"Oh, no worries, I understand completely! Not everyone feels comfortable in such leadership positions, and that is okay! Lillian has done a great job so far leading the project, so I have no doubt that she will be open for the promotion. Anyway, get well soon so that you can come back to work on Monday! We need your brain!"

"Yes, sir, thank you," I whispered, before hanging up the phone.

He would have chosen me. He never thought Lillian was better than me. I just lost the opportunity of a lifetime.

I sat in solitude silence at my kitchen table for a long time, once again coming to terms with the consequences of my choices, and reflecting on what might have been.

WHAT NOT TO DO:
- ❑ Underestimate your own abilities.

ADVICE:
- ❑ Achieving something you want might mean you have to step outside your comfort zone.
- ❑ Stay focused on your strengths, not your weaknesses.

    Don't let others sway your confidence.

EXAMPLES OF GREATNESS

Mark Zuckerberg was born into a middle class family in Dobbs Ferry, New York. From childhood he had a passion and talent for computers and programming. After a run of not so successful ventures, he began working on his next project: a little website called facebook.com. Despite his business niche being occupied by giants like Friendster or MySpace, he persevered when others would have turned away. He set lofty goals of creating an open information flow for all people that would overtake all other social media. He dropped out of Harvard shortly after he saw Facebook's potential.

Since then he has been named the youngest billionaire in US history, including such accreditations as TIME magazine's 2010 Person of the Year, number one on Vanity Fair's 2010 list of Most Influential People of the Information Age, and number sixteen on New Statesman's World's Most Influential Figures list . . . Mark's accolades are many.

Zuckerberg became the youngest billionaire ever because he recognized an opportunity, took advantage of it, and thought, "Why not me?"

Michael Dell's interest in computers started in high school and followed him into college, where he made money on the side putting together customized computers for classmates. That interest grew and became his passion. Despite what family and friends advised him to do, he followed his vision.

He had average grades in high school, dropped out of college, and was told he would never go anywhere. But at age twenty-seven, Michael Dell was named the youngest CEO on the Fortune 500 list. Among his many accolades are PC Magazine's Man of the Year and Chief Executive Magazine's Chief Executive of the Year. He became the CEO of a billion-dollar computer company by asking himself, "Why not me?"

Oprah Winfrey started out with almost nothing. She had no father, was raped at age nine, became pregnant at fourteen and lost the baby two weeks after his birth, and was sent to live in a foster home in New York City. Today she is the richest and most admired and influential African American woman in the world. She created the most successful talk show in history and continues to inspire millions of people in their daily lives, but Oprah's grand legacy exists because she said, "Why not me?"

Howard Stern was born to working class parents in a middle-class neighborhood. From a young age he was conditioned to think that he would not succeed in life. As he got older and discovered his serious interest in radio, people told him that he did not have the voice or the personality to make it as a radio disc jockey.

The Howard Stern Show gained a peak audience of 20 million in sixty markets across the United States and Canada. It was rated the number one morning show in New York from 1994 to 2001. He went on to expand into television that included late-night shows, pay-per-view specials, and home video releases. He is the author of Private Parts and Miss America, both remaining more than fifteen weeks on The New York Times Best Seller list. He created a movie that grossed over $41 million in the United States alone. He signed a deal in 2006 with Sirius Satellite Radio for a reported $500 million and a second one five years later for an undisclosed amount.

Stern made himself an icon despite mediocre beginnings and the criticism he faced because he did what no others dared to do. He made his own opportunities, and he still says, "Why not me?"

Our deepest fear is not that we are inadequate. Our deepest
*   fear is that we are powerful beyond measure.*
It is our light, not our darkness, that most frightens us.
We ask ourselves, Who am I to be brilliant, gorgeous,
*   talented, fabulous?*
Actually, who are you not to be?

Nelson Mandela

MISSED OP:
Supplement Business Failure

My friend and I were always into exercise and nutrition. We workout religiously and kept up-to-date on all the latest nutrition and supplement research.

One day, about ten years ago, as we studied the ingredients on my latest cutting edge purchase, one that we had researched a great deal, we realized that there were only a few ingredients listed on the back of the bottle, ones that were readily available from wholesalers.

I always had an entrepreneurial mind about starting a business. So after some additional research, my friend became my partner and we decided that it was possible to duplicate this new supplement and create a new niche business.

The key to this particular supplement was that it was new to the market, it had a lot of hype around it, and only one company was manufacturing it.

We decided to jump in and cash in on this new craze. We started a business and got on our way. We researched the best ingredients, learned everything we could in this field. We read all the medical papers on what this supplement was supposed to do.

We created a website, business cards, label, business logo; everything was lined up and ready to go.

We double- and triple-checked to make sure everything was in line and ready to be manufactured.

Months went by as we prepared and prepped our business and product for its launch.

Everything was ready to go. But we hesitated. Were we overlooking some fatal flaw? Did we choose the right bottles and labels? Were we charging too much? Too little? Did we do everything correctly?

By the time we finally launched our product, so much time had passed that other companies were joining the fad of this new product.

Then the major manufacturing companies caught wind and they rushed to market.

Instead of being the first one out of the gate, we struggled to grab the scraps the larger companies were leaving behind.

Needless to say, we were squeezed out of the market and lost pretty much our entire investment.

What hurt the most wasn't the lost money or pride. It was that we second-guessed ourselves through the entire process and put doubts in each other's head. That is why our business failed. If only we had acted faster and believed in our choices and decisions, things could have turned out much differently than they did.

WHAT NOT TO DO:
❐ Doubt your own abilities.

ADVICE:
❐ Time moves on with or without you. If you don't take action on your opportunities, someone else will.
❐ Too much preparation can hurt as much as too little preparation.

NO ONE IS BORN INTO GREATNESS

People are born into wealth, power, and privilege, but no one is born into greatness. People are not born with an innate set of skills that makes them successful. Success principles are learned through experience, focus, and practice.

British-based researchers Michael J. Howe, Jane W. Davidson, and John A. Sloboda performed an extensive study on possessing innate gifts that make people extraordinary. Their conclusion?

"The evidence we have surveyed ... does not support the notion that excelling is a consequence of possessing innate gifts." [11]

In other words, they found no direct evidence of high-level performance without experience, focus, and practice. So don't invoke the excuse that you do not possess natural-born talents such as people skills, a keen eye for investing money, a great golf game, or the ability to lose weight or solve problems. Those are learned skills that can be practiced and mastered.

We are not saying that people aren't born with talents in particular areas. Many are. But there is a significant difference between being born into greatness and having a genetic advantage.

The point is that greatness isn't handed to anyone; it requires a lot of hard work coupled with motivation, practice, focus, and the willingness to make or capitalize on opportunities.

People often say that motivation doesn't last.
Well, neither does bathing—that's why we
recommend it daily.

Zig Ziglar

Wasting Time Versus Investing Time

– 8 –

The concept of time is difficult to grasp, even for experts, ranging from quantum physicists and theologians to ancient philosophers. The best they can do is suggest theories about the origin of time, but no one has a complete explanation for this mysterious phenomenon.

Time is represented through change, such as the seasons of the year or the movement of the moon around Earth. Because time is continuous and steady, we use it to mark our calendars and set our clocks. As far as psychology is concerned, our experience of time can be altered by certain significant events. Sit on a park bench on a pretty day and you might forget about time altogether . . . until the sun is setting and you don't know where the day went. But lie on a bunk bed in a jail cell and the passage of a few minutes might seem like an eternity.

Fortunately, the idea of time is not all that complicated for our everyday purposes. We use it to measure the passage of events, opportunities, and our lives. Each of us has seven days a week, twenty-four hours in a day, and sixty minutes per hour. Most important to keep in mind is that time marches on and never pauses or retreats. How we spend time is critical and warrants a closer examination.

In terms of our inner lives, no time exists except
for what is happening in the present moment.

Joan Halifax Roshi

TIME'S VALUE

Once time is used, it can never be retrieved. Time is the most valuable, nonrenewable commodity. Time is priceless because it cannot be duplicated, manufactured, or earned, yet without it we can accomplish nothing. People may worship cash or gold as their most valuable economic assets, but without time, all the money in the world is useless and worthless. No matter how many opportunities are available, or how much power, wealth, and resources we may have at our disposal, if we have no time everything adds up to zero, zilch, nada.

By the same token, if you spend all your money, invest it poorly, or wake up one morning penniless and destitute, you still have a chance to earn more and grow rich with time on your side. But once you spend a minute of your time, it is gone forever, so those who are wise carefully invest their limited amount of time.

We can use time for any number of activities that may yield profoundly positive results, or we can squander it, leaving nothing to show for days, years, or decades of our lives. For that reason we cannot place a dollar amount on the ways we spend our free time. Therefore, always weigh the value of time spent on any activity against the return on your investment, whether watching television, working on your car, walking the dog, or setting new goals.

Ask yourself, "Is this activity worth a resource so precious that it is gone forever after one single use and cannot be bought back with all the money on Wall Street?"

What is it worth to watch a sunset or spend time with loved ones? What is it worth to visualize where you want to be in life this time next year? What is it worth to pursue an opportunity that may get you closer to your dreams? Is it worth it to spend countless hours doing activities that have no relevance to your lifelong goals and will not do anything to advance you toward your dreams?

Also ask, "What is my time worth to others?" If a little bit of your time could positively affect and enhance the life of another human being, what is that worth? Remember, only you can give your time, so what you give is uniquely connected with you as an individual. Time with your family is special to them. Donating your time to a charitable organization may be much more valuable than making a financial contribution. How much is it worth to see a smile on the face of someone you helped? What is your time worth, and how are you going to budget and spend it?

TIME AS AN INVESTMENT

Because time is valuable, we must consider it the same way we think of finances. Return on investment, a term we generally hear in relation to business and accounting, also applies to time. To get a return on an investment essentially means to get something back from it. Likewise, we should try to maximize the returns we get from every hour we spend.

Keep in mind that every single thing we do is an investment of time. We spend it on entertainment when we watch a movie for a couple hours. But if the movie wasn't enjoyable, we did not get a positive return on our investment.

If you condition yourself to think of time as a commodity, something you pay for or trade for other things of value, then all of your actions and activities become investment-based decisions. The goal is to invest your time for the greatest and most rewarding returns. Making those kinds of wise investment choices, even regarding ordinary routines and everyday activities, can propel you forward toward your ultimate dreams and goals.

Look for activities that have the potential to give you more than one return on your investment. An example would be working in a field of interest where you earn income, one kind of beneficial return, while simultaneously working toward your larger lifelong goals, another valuable return. A detailed example might be a person who loves to watch movies and lands a job as a movie critic. He is doing something that is pleasurable and getting paid at the same time. Someone who loves to travel and also likes working with computers might combine the two interests by investing time as a computer technician for a multinational company that flies her all over the globe to troubleshoot computer issues. Discovering activities where multiple positive actions intersect may be more difficult in some cases, but if you manage to succeed it will be well worth the extra effort. Investing time in this intelligent manner lets you hit two birds with one stone, as the old saying goes.

Sadly, the majority of people don't think their time is valuable and do not invest it the way they do their money. They waste it on pursuits that do not further their goals, or on activities that don't mean much to them. The truth is time is the most important asset you have, and it is the one resource you can always invest to help you pursue opportunities, strive toward goals, and reach your lifelong dreams.

Time is free, but it's priceless. You can't own it, but you can use it. You can't keep it, but you can spend it. Once you've lost it you can never get it back.

Harvey MacKay

THE FOUR P'S

How many hours in a day do you waste? We spend time in many different ways: at work or school, sleeping, eating, recreation, entertainment, and so on. But we often use time on activities that fail to bring us profit, preparation, pleasure, or help in the pursuit of our goals. If we stick to investing time according to the four P's, however, we will lead a more rewarding and productive life.

Profit

Time may be your most valuable commodity, but profit is definitely high on the list in terms of importance. Money is a necessity and is probably the best labor-saving device in the world. Going to work, starting a business, or investing in stocks or real estate all share the same goal: monetary profit.

Profits can pay for pleasures in life, or fund you in ways that free you to invest your time in more lucrative activities and more meaningful pursuits. So profit is a powerful component of the four P's, and investing time to gain financial profits is a wise strategy.

Preparation

Preparing for potential opportunities, or at least researching the opportunities that turn up or you create, is another truly wise investment of time. Any goal or objective in life is easier to achieve if you do the right preparation, so spending time in working toward reaching your dreams is generally a high-return investment.

For example, if your goal is to travel across Europe, learn a new language or two—even if you have no idea when or how you'll ever get to Europe. Knowing the language may turn out to be your ticket. Because you speak the lingo, you increase your chances of making friends from there who may invite you over for a visit. Likewise, you improve your potential for landing a job with a company that needs an employee fluent in a foreign language to work in their European branch.

If you want to become active in the stock market but don't have the capital to invest, research companies that have potential, look at stock trends, and track a make-believe portfolio of stocks you'd buy if you had the funds. Once you have the capital saved, you'll be better equipped to capitalize on opportunities, and along the way you'll hone skills as an amateur stock analyst that might help you get a job as a stockbroker.

Looking for the perfect mate? Why not join a gym, take dancing lessons, and research lots of romantic places to go on a dream date? Then when the opportunity to date someone knocks on your door, you'll be full of confidence because you are in good physical shape and look your best. You'll have some dance moves and some great ideas for places to go to have a wonderful time.

If you have nothing on the horizon, consider your interests and explore them further. Start researching and learn about all aspects of those things you're passionate about, because this will often lead to opportunities. You might network with people who can help you get where you want to be, for example, or you might read something about a job opening in your area of interest. Lots of people take classes because they want to learn something new, and some wind up getting hired because of an ad they see on the classroom bulletin board. Or they meet someone in class who is doing the same thing they want to do and needs a business partner or employee.

Pleasure

Everyone needs to unwind and relax by doing something pleasurable. Taking part in activities you enjoy relieves stress, rejuvenates the mind, and reinvigorates your body. A healthy balance of work and play will keep you fresh and motivated so that you can work hard in a sustainable way to reach your lifelong objectives. Sitting in a trance in front of the television for hours and hours does not, however, fall into this category. Watching your favorite TV show or televised sporting event might give you pleasure, of course, and that's a fine activity that delivers real pleasure. But zoning out in front of the tube for hours on end, mindlessly exposing yourself to whatever happens to be on, is a total waste of time. That's a habit or time investment to abandon so that you can instead use those precious hours deriving genuine pleasure from something more rewarding.

Pursuit

Pursuing your goals and opportunity is a must for success. Becoming successful means you have accomplished all of the goals you have set out to do, or at least many of them. But it takes time to actively pursue those goals. So another great way to spend time is to pursue your smaller goals that get you closer to your larger goals and increase your odds of success.

WORK IN YOUR FIELD OF INTEREST

A great way to learn about a career path, profession, or industry is from others who have been there and done that. Then you can use their firsthand experience as your own. An even better approach, however, is to experience that area of interest for yourself—as long as your research concludes that it is a wise investment of your time, as discussed earlier.

To do this, take a position in, or close to, the field of your choice so you can learn what it takes to become successful in that area. You gain valuable inside information by learning about the day-to-day operations, how the industry works, and what kinds of skills and education are needed for business success or career advancement.

This is a main component of the concept of investing time wisely versus wasting time. Take advantage of this strategy if you are thinking of a career change or are unemployed or young and just entering the workforce. If you have a full schedule already, maybe you can work part-time. If a company or particular field does not offer part-time employment, ask to volunteer. You can even do this when the job market seems tight, because everyone needs free help.

Internship is usually reserved for young college kids as part of their education credentials, but it is not limited to them. You might even apprentice for minimum wage or for nothing at all, no matter what your age or status. Once you get in, work hard. People will notice if you do an outstanding job, especially when you're not getting paid for it. Be patient. If you cannot afford to invest your time longer than a few weeks or months, then it's possible your hard work will pay off and the business owner or manager might offer you a permanent, paid position to keep you on. At the very least, he or she will likely provide you with valuable, excellent job references.

Before you call me crazy and close the book for suggesting that you work for free, remember to keep an open mind. What are a couple of weeks or months to you if you are investing in learning about a field you're passionate about? Consider it the price of tuition in the school of personal experience. Ask someone who is miserable in his job if he wishes he had worked in this position beforehand, while he had the flexibility to make other career choices. Investing time to learn about your potential career field is not a waste, even if you have to do it for free. You might find that your career path is everything you dreamed it would be. Or you might discover that, although it looked glamorous from the outside, it is not what you thought it would be. It is better to gain that insightful realization before you put all your eggs into one basket and risk hard work, precious time, and your entire future on something that is not right for you.

The more informed you are, the more you can focus your efforts on achieving your own dreams and goals. In addition to learning about your field of interest and discovering what is required to succeed, you will also be making important connections and creating professional networks with people in positions to help you. They may also introduce you to other opportunities you didn't know about before you entered the field.

WASTING TIME

Many time management experts define wasting time as doing anything that does not contribute to the accomplishment of your goals. I tend to define it as doing anything that doesn't generate a profit, give you genuine pleasure, or prepare you for opportunities in pursuit of your goals. Time spent outside those areas is wasted and lost.

Think about the fact that there are entire websites designed to get people to visit them and waste time. Meanwhile, behind those sites are clever people who take advantage of all that wasted time by making tons of money on advertising posted on those sites.

Have you ever been bored while unemployed, so you sat at home watching afternoon television like The Jerry Springer Show? Have you noticed that the advertisements during that kind of show target people who are broke and unemployed? That's where most of the get-rich-quick schemes are advertised, and where you'll be encouraged to pawn your car title in exchange for a little more money that you can spend on pizza, beer, and the monthly cable bill. The advertisers make a killing, while the viewers space-out on the sofa, feeling like losers. Nothing positive comes from that kind of wasted time, and it often leads to lower self-esteem or feelings of depression.

Evolve your thinking so that you realize spending time in this way is a crazy idea. Let's face it. If you cannot think of something better to do than watch mindless online videos of a teen trying to break the world record of how many shirts he can wear at once, you will not experience amazing success and extraordinary dream fulfillment.

If you're at home, invest time intelligently. When you're on the job, put your whole heart into it. If you cannot bring yourself to do that, then research something that will educate you or prepare you for a job you'll enjoy. If you're wasting time in a relationship, fix it or get out of it, for your sake and your partner's. Move on and make progress instead of wasting time in an unhealthy and stagnant situation.

Live each act of life as if it was your last, and you will start to put 100 percent of your effort into whatever you are doing. You won't waste another second, because you'll be living your life as if every moment is a precious gift—which it is.

MISSED OP:
A Second Chance

My name is Paul Peterson, just your average everyday guy working in New York City. I didn't go to college, but I had some decent common sense, or so I thought, which allowed me to get a job as an elevator technician in a New York City high-rise apartment complex.

My job wasn't glamorous by any means, but I took some pride in my work. Yet something was always missing. I wished that I'd had the chance to go to college, but money was always an issue in my family. I felt a bit stuck.

Then one day things went from bad to worse. While working I accidentally tripped and fell, twisting my knee in a very awkward way. The pain was immediate and intense. I knew that I wouldn't be able to keep doing my job, and I panicked about how I could support myself and my family.

What's worse is that hurting my knee had a little bit to do with being out of shape. So I was mad at myself for not paying attention and letting myself go. I had a lot of time to think about that because, luckily for me, my company paid for my sick leave.

My doctors warned me that going back to work right away wouldn't be a good idea, but they weren't really specific about how long I needed to stay home. At first, I thought that it would just be a week or two.

During that first two weeks I felt pretty sorry for myself. So I spent my time watching TV, playing video games and sleeping quite a bit. My wife, Sarah, and our two kids, Ben and Cindy, didn't like it much. I was getting paid, though, so they couldn't really complain too much.

Fairly soon I realized that I would probably be out of work for several months. I thought about what I should do with that time. I could maybe take a college class. I could join a gym and do some light exercises on everything but my knee to keep myself in shape. I could even do some little home improvement projects that I had been meaning to get to.

They were all good thoughts, but the laziness kept creeping back in. Besides, it was fun to play games and watch TV and not have to worry about anything. I was acting like a retiree and enjoying every minute of it.

Meanwhile, Sarah was getting increasingly frustrated with me. She and I would argue on a regular basis about my attitude. That was the only real problem, or so I thought. Then, after about a year, my two kids came to me and said that they were really worried about me. They said that all I seemed to care about was my TV. I was gaining weight, eating junk food, and not spending time with them anymore.

That should have been my wake-up call. I should have taken the two of them out into the backyard and pushed Cindy on her swing set and tossed a ball around with Ben. Instead, I told them that I'd love for them to sit and play video games with me.

I might have noticed the disappointment in my little girl's eyes more if Ben hadn't been grinning from ear to ear at the thought of playing games with dear old dad. He sat down and we played video games together for three hours. I thought we were having a great time.

After that, my arguments with my wife escalated. She told me that she couldn't stand to see little Cindy upset. She also said that I was being an awful influence on Ben. He wasn't doing his homework anymore and he was eating too much junk and playing too many games.

Well, three years after my knee injury, the company quit paying for me to stay home. I knew I was better. I had been better for ages, but I had no reason to go back to work or do anything. It came as a bit of a shock when they told me that my money was going to be cut off.

The night before I started back to work in the high-rise apartment building, I lay in bed, talking to my wife. "It's about time!" she said.

Well, it really was all about time, but not in the way that Sarah meant. I was finally starting to feel the weight of all of that wasted time. I was overweight, I was tired, I was going back to the same dead-end job after three years of doing nothing. I couldn't believe that I had done that to myself.

What's worse is that I did it to my family. Cindy would barely talk to me, Sarah and I were not on the same page anymore, and Ben and I got along fine, but only because he was following in my lazy footsteps. All in all, my life was a mess.

The worst of all was that three years had gone by and I had absolutely nothing positive to show for it. Neither did my family. We could have done so many things together. Not only that, but I could have gone back to school while I was injured. I might have even had a better paying job by now, which would have taken some of the financial pressure off of my wife.

I was a miserable man that night, and I've been a miserable man ever since. I wasted far too much time and wasted a huge opportunity in the process. How many working adults get a real chance to have that much time off? I could have started my life over or accomplished so much. I'm always going to wonder what I could have done with my life during that time instead of squandering it away.

WHAT NOT TO DO:
❏ Squander your free time away.

ADVICE:
❏ Be active and try to live a healthy lifestyle.
❏ Keep working toward your goals and ambitions.
❏ Use your free time wisely.

Wasted time comes in many forms. So go after what you want and don't settle for less just because it is the easier thing to do. In the end you might look back and realize what looked easy was actually a lot harder and delivered disappointing results.

Do not squander time, for that is the stuff life is made of.

Benjamin Franklin

REMEMBER . . .

Working for a short time in a particular field to research it and gain hands-on experience can lead to success and additional opportunities and options, even before you decide whether or not to commit to it. Do the research on what it is you want to accomplish. Take the time to explore all aspects of your goals and objectives in advance. Do more in the time you are given, and find activities that you can cut out or modify to make more time for the important things in life. It is often smarter to invest time before making a long-term decision.

Booze Bets and Babies

—9—

Most people do not have a long-range plan or lifetime strategy, so they float along with no real sense of purpose or consistent motivation. They are like jellyfish that is tossed by the waves, eventually washing up wherever the tides take them.

Experts estimate that approximately 97 percent of all people do not have written goals, and it is no surprise that these same people do not consider themselves successful. In other words, the vast majority of people spend more time planning their yearly vacations then they do planning their lives. Even before heading off to the supermarket or home improvement store, most people first make a list of things they need so they don't forget something. Yet they won't bother to write down their goals for life. But without being focused on goals in clear-cut, tangible ways, they won't see the opportunities to achieve them.

Knowledge and hard work don't magically create the desired result without also applying focus, concentration, and intent. You may work like a mule and have multiple diplomas, but without first identifying your goals, you won't recognize the opportunities that can take you where you want to go. Without clear direction it is just too easy to become derailed, distracted, or dispersed into lots of different directions.

If writing down goals is the key to successful goal setting, and if setting goals represents the foundation for success, then why do only three or four people out of every 100 write down their goals and revisit them on a consistent basis? Coaches write down the plays they want their teams to execute to win the game. Successful students write down their homework assignments and take notes during class. Entrepreneurs submit written business plans to get bank loans. Before making hotel and car rental reservations, itineraries are planned. But somehow most of us don't grasp the importance of setting goals related to the really big, important dreams we cherish.

Maybe it's because we might feel embarrassed if someone glimpsed our list of goals and dreams and made fun of it. They might snicker at the loftiness of our goals or deride us for believing that we can do what others consider impossible.

But people will put you down for thinking big because they lack self-confidence. They impose their self-limiting beliefs through criticism and instill doubt and disbelief because they don't want you to get ahead while they get nowhere in life. Do not let doubters and naysayers adversely influence your pursuit of success. Prove them wrong or die trying. That will guarantee that you live your life to the fullest, on your own terms, with passion. Just doing that is a remarkable and heroic achievement.

Most people don't want to write down their plans because they are afraid of failing to achieve them. Keeping things vague protects us from being accountable for missing the mark. When we write down something, we commit ourselves to it. Failing to live up to what one has affirmed for himself can be disheartening, so people are often scared of explicitly stating their goals. But knowing how to fail and learning from experience is an attribute shared by all truly successful people. Don't be afraid to dream, and remember that early failure can sometimes be the precursor of later, greater success.

Occasionally people don't set goals for another unfortunate reason: they lack the inner desire to want something greater out of life. They have been conditioned to accept a mediocre life and a subpar lifestyle. They are content to conform and be like hamsters on society's multilane treadmill.

But whatever it is that's holding you back and keeping you in that 97 percent of the population that has hang-ups, reservations, or fears—and no written, accountable, and concrete plan for the future—today is the day for you to step it up and hop off the treadmill to nowhere. Become a member of that rare 3 percent who will attain their dreams and be successful beyond their wildest imaginations simply because they acknowledged, defined, and passionately pursued their lifetime goals.

A goal that is casually set and lightly taken
will be freely abandoned at the first obstacle.

Zig Ziglar

AVOID DERAILMENT; HAVE A PLAN

If you set off to drive from New York to Los Angeles without a road map, it would be safe to say that you would get lost at some point, maybe even before you get out of the Big Apple. So why try to navigate life without a map or plan?

With a lifelong plan in place, you are much less likely to veer off course or be detoured or distracted. It is almost inevitable that without goals you will go off in a different direction than you had in mind. This is why so many people look back over their lives and see themselves in a totally different position and place than they had envisioned and intended when they started their journey through adulthood.

When a major event or obstacle pops up in one's path, he must decide how to get past it. But with no goals and plans to follow, it is too easy to make choices in the moment that shift the direction ever so gradually. Life is full of decisions and choices, so by straying slightly, even by a degree or two, a person will end up completely turned around over the course of a lifetime. Over steer by just an eighth of an inch and see how long it takes to drive your car into the nearest ditch.

For example, let's say you are hit with an unplanned pregnancy. You will have to make hurried decisions about life that would normally warrant deliberate and patient consideration. Maybe you have to put college on hold or forego it completely. One out of every four dropouts leaves school because of pregnancy/child rearing.[12] You might accept a crummy job with low pay because you need money fast, giving up the chance at a great career. Perhaps you were saving for a down payment on a home, but now that money will need to be used for the baby.

This situation creates another obstacle if you are not married or committed to your partner. This pregnancy inextricably attaches and connects you to someone you intended only to date for a short time before you continued looking for the girl or guy of your dreams. A summer fling can turn into a lifetime commitment of caring for a child you both share responsibility for parenting. In addition, you are also now attached to a child! Even if you break up with your partner, you are still a parent, connected to your child, as is the child's other parent. Your child needs both mother and father. Then you meet someone special, the one you've waited for all your life. But you bring a child into that relationship, and, fair or unfair, that person may not want to get involved with someone with this kind of baggage from a previous relationship.

The point is to try and avoid situations that will cause you to deviate from your plan. If a life changing unexpected event does happen, like an unplanned pregnancy, be ready to adjust to the situation and get back on track. Look at the opportunity in having a child: perhaps it will be the motivation you need to push you to create a better life for yourself and your newborn.

My wife and I faced this situation. Once I realized that Caryn was pregnant, it was too late for hindsight to do me any good. Instead of following my own well-strategized blueprint for success and goal fulfillment, I had to adapt to the circumstances laid at my doorstep and adjust to make the most of it.

Even if you have thoughtfully and purposefully mapped out your goals and how you will reach them, life's obstacles—sickness, death, broken relationships, etc.—have the potential to radically alter your life plan. These are physically, sometimes financially, and certainly emotionally charged obstacles. They hit planners and seat-of-the-pantsers alike. The people with a well-defined roadmap will recover from setbacks more quickly because of their planning; the ones without a clear plan are likely to continue drifting in whatever direction the obstacle has sent them.

DROPOUTS

As a matter of fact, well-defined goals are so important that if high school or college dropouts had solid written game plans for life, they would have several more options available to them. There are plenty of examples of people who dropped out of school but continued to pursue their plans and become highly successful. On the other hand, there are hardly any success stories about dropouts who left school without a clue as to what they wanted from life.

Statistically speaking, students who dropped out of high school have a negative effect on the economy. We don't mean just the personal finances or earning power of individuals who drop out. The yearly cost to American taxpayers adds up to about $8 billion in public assistance programs to support or subsidize dropouts,[13] and high school dropouts earn about $10,000 less per year than workers with diplomas. [13] Dropouts are more likely to be unemployed and incarcerated: the majority of inmates in federal prisons are high school dropouts.[14]

Teachers and schools cannot be held accountable if their students are not self-motivated. A survey of 500 dropouts aged 16 to 25 found that almost 70 percent left school because they were not motivated to do schoolwork. [12] If this kind of student can be helped to see the connection between formal education and attainment of personal dreams, the dropout rate could be substantially reduced. This requires that students learn to create goals they can relate to, focus on, and follow, because once they see the roadmap to a more amazing future, they will likely better understand how education is an extremely vital aspect of their lifelong journeys.

Accomplishing self-imposed goals is both intrinsically and extrinsically motivating, and it can help reduce the number of dropouts around the world, which will benefit all of us. If you have already dropped out, take this opportunity to get on a track that will help you achieve what you want out of life.

ONE MISTAKE CAN EXPONENTIALLY MULTIPLY

One mistake can lead to another, and then each of those has the potential to branch off and multiply. Soon you find yourself entangled in several errors and regrets. That original misstep or poor judgment call can also result in intensified repercussions. Mistakes happen, but even minor ones can compound until they have a devastating negative impact on your life, whether you are young or old.

If you are not following a well-designed plan to keep your eyes on the prize, your big career dreams could easily get derailed. You might lose sight of your goals and wind up at the wrong party or in the wrong car, mixed up with the wrong crowd and end up with an arrest record that limits you in many areas of life. You might have had too much alcohol, get behind the wheel of a car, and be involved in a fatal accident. You could go to jail for, drinking while intoxicated, reckless driving or vehicular manslaughter. Mistakes made intentionally or unintentionally can put your lifelong dreams in jeopardy, and blemishes on your criminal history can haunt you as stubborn, difficult-to-overcome obstacles for the rest of your life.

But it's not necessary to have something as dramatic as a bankruptcy, car wreck, drug bust, or unwanted pregnancy to totally trash your hopes and dreams and wreak havoc in your life. Even something as commonplace and socially acceptable as a lack of fundamental health and wellness can lead to disastrous consequences. Bad health creates a powerful kind of debt that taxes your body and inflicts chronic distress that can physically impoverish you.

Following an unhealthy lifestyle is easy to do, especially when you are young and carefree and surrounded by adult role models who eat junk food, don't get enough sleep or exercise, and invite all kinds of daily stress into their existence as normal and ordinary. Most Americans lead essentially unhealthy lives, but just because everyone else is doing it does not mean that you must blindly follow them down that unhappy and unwholesome path.

Seemingly simple acts of smoking, drinking, eating food that lacks nutrition, not exercising, engaging in unprotected sex, or abusing recreational drugs have the potential to produce an unhealthy body and a dull mind. Follow an unhealthy lifestyle over the course of many years and the damage is compounded. Plus whenever you get sick because of your unhealthy condition, it costs you in doctor bills and time missed from work. Some of these problems surface early; others don't manifest until you are older. But all of them eventually catch up with you and inflict misery.

The good news is that the human body and mind are extremely resilient, and plenty of resources are available to help you live a more balanced and healthy life. Even after many years of punishing and abusing your body, you can rehabilitate an unhealthy, disease-prone lifestyle and change your habits, replacing detrimental behaviors with positive ones that give you extra energy, stamina, and feelings of confidence (see Chapter 6). You can actually improve your outward appearance and literally add years to your life by just getting healthier and seeking balance and wellness.

If you are not pleased with your current state of health, it's never too late to change. You have plenty of time to make dramatic, uplifting, and rewarding changes, which will pay you rich dividends in multidimensional ways for years to come.

To keep your life on track and your goals and dreams front and center, observe what others around you have gone through that caused them to miss their big opportunities. Carefully consider how they regretted the erroneous or ill-conceived decisions they made earlier in life. Use other people's mistakes and detrimental detours to equip you with the knowledge of when to make better choices, how to upgrade your circumstances, and what steps to take now to reach your dreams in time to fully live them to your heart's content.

MISSED OP:
Forced Decisions

The Friday night before Memorial Day weekend 1997, I was at my best friend's house getting ready for the holiday. Billy and I were both single and just looking to have a good time. We were excited about all the things we were going to do that summer: travel, attend parties at Fire Island, take trips to the Hamptons and New York City, enjoy fun in the surf and sun.

Then it happened. Beep! Beep! Beep! Beep! My pager went off, and the number coming across the screen belonged to Caryn, the woman I had been dating. I called her to find out what the heck was so urgent, not expecting to hear news that would entirely change not only the trajectory of my summer but also the journey across the rest of my life. Caryn was pregnant, and we both knew without a shadow of a doubt that I was the father. What was to be the most free and easy summer ever suddenly became the most stressful and hardest few months of my life.

At the time I owned a landscaping business with my brothers. Although it was lucrative, I didn't have health insurance, and I certainly didn't envision myself being a lifelong landscaper. I was saving money and considering options as to what to do with the rest of my life. I didn't have to decide anything right away and I had plenty of time on my side. Then I got the news that I was going to be a father and my whole reality shifted. Not only did I have to quickly figure out how to take care of a wife and baby, but I was going to have a wife and a baby! How could this have happened? For a guy who seemed to have it all put together, how could I have let something like this happen? How could I have been so irresponsible? How many times had this story played out before: someone with great potential had their grand plans derailed by an unplanned event?

It's not like I didn't have the opportunity to prevent this from happening. Even though I had plenty of examples from others around me, I didn't choose to use their experiences as my own, I still slipped up. Because of that "slip," my options for that summer and the rest of my life had become limited in ways I never expected.

WHAT NOT TO DO:

❑ Think a particular situation will never happen to you.

ADVICE:

❑ If you are not ready for children or a family of your own, take precautions.

❑ Follow your list of life goals and stay on track.

❑ If an unplanned event occurs adapt, adjust, and overcome to get back on track.

SITUATIONAL AWARENESS

Evaluate every situation and beware of those circumstances that can derail you. Constantly scan the horizon for signs of trouble so you will see mistakes coming your way and avoid them before they have a chance to ambush your plans.

Here are some key areas to be aware of as you move forward toward your objectives:

Live Debt Free

The best way to ensure financial stability is to stay out of debt, and the easiest way to prevent debt is to avoid overspending. Don't live beyond your financial means. Don't spend more money than you make or rely on borrowing other people's money to pave your way. Put yourself on a budget. Give yourself a set amount of cash each week, like a parent gives a child an allowance. Once it's spent, don't spend any more. Replace pastimes that cost money with inexpensive or free activities. Wait before buying a high-ticket item. Don't rush out and purchase it right away. Oftentimes during the wait, the item will lose its importance and allure. Research to make sure you're getting the best deal. Buy things when they go on sale or ones that are gently pre-owned, have retained their value, and are being sold in great condition but at a discounted price.

Avoid Unplanned Pregnancy

Practice safe sex and birth control or abstinence until you are ready to parent a child. Thoroughly familiarize yourself with the many different methods of birth control and the effectiveness of each one. Talk to your partner about birth control and your plans for having children or not having them. If you're unable to talk with them about this sensitive topic, visit a counselor who can facilitate the discussion and make it more comfortable for both of you to openly communicate. Remember that no birth control is 100 percent effective and if a pregnancy does happen look how that obstacle can turn into an opportunity.

Don't Do Drugs

Alcohol, nicotine, and illegal as well as prescription drugs can all be highly addictive. I call these "multiple negatives" because they have several negative effects, not just one. They rob you of your health, energy, money, and sometimes your friends and family. Long term drug use saps your motivation and drive for success. Drugs tear apart your health both mentally and physically. Doing drugs lowers your inhibitions and decision-making ability and may lead to other unwanted problems with the law, your job, or relationships. If you have an addictive personality, stay away from them completely because they will suck you in like a black hole. If you are already hooked and dependent, seek help and support today to break the cycle and habit and resume a life of independence and freedom. With years of previous experience in drug enforcement, I could write novels just on the destruction and failure that drug use and distribution leave behind. I have seen firsthand how drugs can ruin a person's life financially, emotionally, and physically. There is no larger obstacle to a successful life than letting drugs derail your goals, camouflage opportunity, and ruin your future.

Don't Get Arrested

This is easy for some people but a lot easier said than done for others.

Hanging around the wrong type of people is usually the main cause of legal trouble, so evaluate your friends. If they are a magnet for run-ins with the law and can get you into trouble, it is time to find a new crowd. Use reputable business outlets and do research on the people you hire or work for. Many people lose their direction in life and their freedom because they did business with crooks. Use a sound decision-making process when in situations that could get you in trouble. Always ask yourself, "Could this derail my goals or opportunity?"

MISSED OP:
Bad Influences

I always believed Fred would do something noteworthy, something outstanding with his life. When I received the call from my mother to look at that day's newspaper, though, I still found it hard to believe how wrong I'd been.

I was in sixth grade when I met Fred, the boy genius with an IQ rumored to be in the 160s. It was a regular occurrence to see him doing the upper classmen's trigonometry and calculus homework. He said he did it for the extra lunch money, though I suspect he would've done it for free, just to keep his mind challenged.

Being friends with Fred was like being friends with an interactive encyclopedia; he had an answer for every question I asked, even though many of his explanations went right over my head.

Fred always seemed to have people around him. He was a genius, sure, but he wasn't one of those geeky, loner types who surrounded themselves with books and nothing else. People liked Fred because he wasn't arrogant or bossy, didn't seem to think of himself as any better than anyone, even though he was smarter than most adults.

When we got to high school, Fred started attracting the interest of colleges. He went to a few interviews, and the admissions people practically fell over themselves trying to get him to enroll. He received several scholarship offers, all before the eleventh grade. Our school newspaper wrote a profile on him, and even the local paper did a story, highlighting Fred in their "Rising Star" feature, which was usually reserved for a graduating senior.

"So is this the last I'm going to see of you?" I asked Fred one day at lunch. It was our running joke; every time another college tried to woo him with a bigger scholarship, a nicer dorm room, I expected he'd accept the offer and be catapulted to the stratosphere of Ivy League academics. But he remained in the troposphere, in high school, with the rest of us regular kids. He wanted to go to MIT and study Atmospheric and Planetary Sciences, so he'd wait until he was a senior and apply, just like everyone else.

Looking back on it now, it's easy to see what caused Fred's stupendous downfall, though at the time, it seemed like a great fortune had been bestowed upon him: his parents had their basement finished and allowed Fred free reign. It was supposed to be his workshop, of sorts, his studio, his place to go and be brilliant. He'd been talking about building a telescope that summer, and though neither of his parents knew what such an endeavor involved, it sounded like something that needed a lot of space and would probably make a gigantic mess, so the basement became Fred's domain.

Fred's parents went on vacation to their lake house for a month, leaving Fred behind to work on his telescope. Word got around, though, that not only were Fred's parents out of town, but he had his very own space, the entire basement of a house. People now looked up to Fred for a different reason: he could host the biggest parties and no one would worry about the presence of parents.

I went to one of the parties, the first one, not entirely sure what to expect, but when the basement became so clouded with pot smoke that it stung my eyes, I left. I didn't even say good-bye to Fred, whom I saw across the room, laughing so hard no sound came out of his mouth.

The parties continued, though I never went back. Even when Fred's parents returned, people still went over there, albeit in far fewer numbers. I was preoccupied with studying for the AP tests and applying to colleges, so I didn't notice Fred's transformation until it was complete. We had just drifted apart is what I told myself, but the truth of it was Fred was now unrecognizable. All he did was do drugs. He had a group of friends he smoked daily with; they'd sit in his basement and pass an enormous glass pipe around, holding the smoke deep in their lungs until their faces turned bright red. I went over there only once, after Fred's mother called me and asked if I would try to talk to him. "He was always fond of you. You were always such a good friend to him. Please, I don't know what else to do."

But there was nothing for me to do, either. Fred only stared dully at me with bloodshot eyes. Someone said something incomprehensible, and Fred laughed, a hacking sort of croak, and reached for the pipe. I turned and left. What was I supposed to say?

Years passed and two days before I was to graduate college, I was sitting at the table in my small student apartment, once again going over the speech I would give as valedictorian. I'd gone over it so many times it was practically seared into my DNA, but I still felt the need to read the words I'd long since memorized. I was almost done when the phone rang.

"Did you get the paper this morning?" my mother said.

"I haven't been out yet, but I'm sure they delivered it. Why?"

"There's a story I think you should see. About Fred."

I asked her what it was about, but she wouldn't say anything else. So I hung up and trotted down three flights of stairs to the lobby where the delivery boy tossed a handful of plastic-wrapped newspapers each morning. I entertained the possibilities of what this story might be about; it had been so long since I'd last heard anything about Fred, and I hoped whatever article I was about to read would detail Fred's astonishing turnaround, his meteoric rise back to where he was supposed to be, how he lived up to his astronomical potential after all.

Fred's picture was on page three, under a blaring headline: "Four Arrested in Drug Bust." It was one of the largest marijuana seizures in our state, and Fred was charged with possession with intent to distribute, he was looking at spending years in federal prison. I folded the paper under my arm, and on the way back upstairs, I dropped it down the second floor trash chute.

Two days later, I stood at the podium in front of my fellow classmates and bleachers full of their ecstatic parents. I did not recite the speech I planned on. Instead, I spoke of the importance of valuing the gifts we are given, realizing the potential of every opportunity, and using our intellect not just to succeed academically but also to make good choices.

WHAT NOT TO DO:
❐ Get involved with lifestyle that offers little chance
of a positive outcome.

ADVICE:
❐ Determine if your peers are influencing you positively or
negatively. Remove yourself from negative peer-pressure
situations.
❐ Stay away from drugs. They will derail many of your
life goals.

STAYING OUT OF TROUBLE

Even successful people make poor decisions. In November 2010 it was reported that Tiger Woods, the most famous golfer and highest paid athlete in history, had been cheating on his wife. Woods has two children and had been married for six years. The rest of the sordid details you probably already know, and quite frankly they don't matter. The point is that what happened to Woods wasn't accidental; it came about as a result of his poor judgment and, more important, his ultimate decisions.

I am sure that Woods had several opportunities to address potential problems that he and his wife may have had or to just to tell her the truth about what he really wanted, which might have been a divorce. But apparently he did not look at the mistakes of others and use their regrets to direct his own decision-making process. The price tag on that divorce was in the neighborhood of $100 million, and his tarnished image surely cost him much more than that in money lost when companies like Nike, Gatorade, Electronic Arts, TAG Heuer, and Gillette dropped him from their highly lucrative endorsement contracts. In fact, the $100 million he reportedly paid out during the divorce was only about a year's income for Tiger, who had, according to Forbes Magazine, already earned more than $1 billion during his career.

Woods risked all of that because he didn't step back and evaluate his decisions, and the decisions of so many others like him in similar circumstances who also learned the hard way. He didn't make or take the opportunity to evaluate his position, and it cost him big-time.

Former NBA star and TNT NBA analyst Charles Barkley revealed his own struggles with gambling in an interview with ESPN. After being asked about golfer John Daly, who claimed to have lost about $55 million over a twelve-year period due to gambling, Barkley's response was, "Do I have a gambling problem? Yeah, I do have a gambling problem. But I don't consider it a big problem because I can afford to gamble. It's just a stupid habit that I've got to get under control, because it's just not a good thing to be broke after all of these years."

Although Barkley told ESPN that he's working to solve the problem, he added that he gambles too much and he gambles for too much money. Barkley went on. "I think the most difficult thing I've got to realize is that no matter how much I win, it ain't a lot. It's only a lot when I lose, and you always lose."

Analyze what you can learn from others when you hear their stories. When a situation arises, step back, assess the pros and cons, and utilize a solid decision-making process before making a choice about your next step or the next move.

There are myriad ways to take advantage of opportunities, while steering clear of the hazards and pitfalls. But it all comes down to making the right decisions when the time arises, and that brings us full circle, back to the necessity of having concrete, well-articulated goals and subsets of goals that guide us day by day, hour by hour, step by step toward the practical realization of our lifelong dreams.

Why do so many people get themselves into situations that jeopardize their futures? How do we prevent unwanted events from derailing our goals? The answer is simple. Learn from the mistakes other people make, while surrounding yourself with good people to minimize your chances of making mistakes. Before making any decision, first ask yourself, "How can this help or hurt my plans for success?" Go through the decision-making process and choose wisely, based on what will propel you forward instead of holding you back.

Here are some basic principles that will make your journey easier and more fruitful:

Stay Focused

Be consistently focused, though you may have to frequently refocus on your goals as circumstances change and evolve around you. Every day the unexpected and unplanned happens, and that's why it is critical to write down goals and revisit them daily; otherwise, it is much too easy to forget your goals or just simply drift gradually farther from them, like a boat without an anchor quietly moving away from the marina and out into the deep blue sea. Before you know it, your goals will be so far removed from where you find yourself that they are completely out of sight and unreachable.

Keep Busy

One very simple way to stay on track and avoid trouble is to keep busy. As they say, "Idle hands are the Devil's workshop." Keep working toward your goals with staunch determination, staying active and engaged, and you won't have time to get embroiled in erroneous situations and energy-sapping drama.

Appreciate the Value of Others' Blunders

Military tacticians learn as much or more from studying the disastrous defeats that legendary warriors suffered as they do from reading about famous victories and award-winning heroes. Analyzing the mistakes of other people can give you a PhD in the tactics of a successful life. You're reading Missed Ops, so use the examples and case histories presented herein and study the mistakes outlined and illustrated for you in this book. Observe the mistakes of friends and family members, and examine what they did wrong in each unique circumstance. Find other resources to study the blunders of others, using the Internet, books, magazines, movies, or television, and brainstorm how you would have handled those situations differently and better in your own life.

Submerge Yourself in Positivity

Surround yourself with people who are successful and have a positive outlook. Be with those who make good decisions and will help you make better decisions. People with positive influence can help you stay on your path to success, whereas negative influences will put you directly in harm's way. Keep in mind that genuinely good friends are not trying to get you to think or be like them but to be the best possible version of your own unique self.

Interrogate Your Choices

Ask yourself at every decision junction, "Does this have the potential to be an opportunity to move me closer to my goals, or to postpone or harm my plans for the future?" Pay close attention to the answer, whether you like the answer or not, and you will radically improve your chances of success.

Keep Your Decision-Making Process Sharp

Identify and prioritize your objectives. Analyze and make a list of the pros and cons based on thorough due diligence. Make a tentative decision and then further evaluate it, looking for additional possible consequences. Once you finalize your decision take decisive action. Adjust your original decision accordingly, based on new information or evolving circumstances, by being flexible and adaptable (see Chapter 11). Make notes on a calendar when to review your decision. That way you can ensure you are hitting the mileposts and benchmarks you should have clearly laid out when you first identified your goals and assigned the priority to each one.

If you accustom yourself to using these tools on a regular basis, you will develop an automatic methodology that will serve you almost like an instinctual sixth sense to keep you out of trouble and immersed in ongoing successes. Habits are rooted in the subconscious mind, and research has shown that at least 80 percent of our brain power comes from that subconscious level.[14] Repetition is the key to cultivating that potent natural resource, and it is also the most effective way to plant skills in your mind so that they quickly form positive habits and become deeply engrained assets.

Not straying from your path in life is hard work. If it were easy, everyone would be doing it and almost everyone in the world would be wildly successful, while the people writing self-help books and creating self-improvement workshops would be broke and unemployed.

"Just Because" Syndrome

–10–

Lemmings are a rodent that lives in colder climates. They will periodically migrant from one place to another in a large group, and during these mass relocations they basically follow the same route. They are famous for running headlong over cliffs to their deaths because they simply follow what the rest of the crowd does.

So the word lemming has become synonymous with blindly following the crowd. To call others a lemming is a derogatory remark meaning that they have no self-identity or ability to think for themselves. Many people foolishly follow one another "just because" and migrate from one activity or destination to the next, like lemmings, geese, or sheep. But we are not lemmings that mindlessly follow one another over a cliff, nor are we geese that have to migrate together for survival or sheep that herd for protection. So why do so many people act like they are?

For example, going to college is a great goal, but if your only motivation is because everyone else in your high school graduating class is heading off to college, then you need to revisit your goals and analyze your options. Are you going for an education to get you the job you desire, or just to please your parents? Plenty of people go to college, get a job, get married, and have children because they observe other people doing those things. But that does not mean you have to. You can change one or all of those steps, based on your own personal goals, preferences, and passions in life.

For the most part, we are conditioned to repeat what our parents did and what their parents did before them. If that's what you genuinely want, go for it. But it's important for you to understand that it doesn't have to be that way if you don't want it to be. Each person can and absolutely should each choose his or her own path in life, set his or her own goals, and pursue his or her own dreams.

Those goals and dreams will come true only if we know how to plan for them and recognize the opportunities that will get us there. But the path to that kind of success in life is not always going to be the same path that others traveled, including parents, siblings, and friends.

Most people who regret not making better choices or seizing other more favorable opportunities got where they are by blindly accepting the status quo, like a lemming. But human life is not meant for behaving like a lemming or a hamster on a treadmill. Use your intelligence, follow your heart, and learn from the mistakes and regrets of others so that you don't repeat their missteps.

DON'T SETTLE

Don't make life-altering decisions just because it is what's expected of you. In other words, do not settle for any old life; rather, make your life as extraordinary as you want it to be.

Many times people neglect to use an intentional decision-making process, or they don't give much thought to mapping out their life goals. They accept what's handed to them and buy into it. But it's shocking that they wouldn't apply the same nonchalant and meek process to shopping for, say, truck tires or household appliances. As consumers they don't hesitate to visit several stores to get the best price, carefully crunching numbers to ensure the best outcome. They research, consult the experts, ask for recommendations, and construct a comprehensive plan of action to make sure they get the most for their money. If they think they're getting ripped off, they complain or negotiate a better deal.

Yet when it comes to deciding the direction of their lives, which is ultimately the most valuable decision anyone can make, they don't bother to do as much thinking and investigating as they do when they pick out a new television set or buy a used car.

Be fully aware of how futile and unrealistic that is. If you value your life at least as much as you value a washing machine, lawn mower, or laptop, be deliberate about taking control of your destiny. Otherwise you are just going to rip yourself off, sell yourself short, and wind up with regrets.

Don't live your life according to what others expect you to do. Don't choose a career because your guidance counselor or academic advisor told you to. Choose something you're passionate about it and it's what you love the most.

Don't get married just because she has a job and your family likes her. Get married because you love her so much it pains you to be away from her. Don't have children because all of your friends are creating families for themselves. Do it because you are ready and want to bring a child into the world to nurture and love.

Of course, as a seventeen-year-old high school student you cannot expect to know what you want to do with the rest of your life, because you haven't yet had the chance to explore different options and opportunities. Take time to develop a broader and more panoramic outlook. Don't commit to the first career that comes along just because it pays well. You might make money but spend every day miserable, and no amount of money can adequately compensate you for a life of chronic unhappiness.

In other chapters we discuss various ways to outline goals and action plans. But in this chapter we implore you to honestly ask yourself if those objectives are actually your own goals and dreams. We want to discourage you from making any particular plans just because society says you should. Instead, we want to encourage you to make a life plan that is uniquely yours, and one you genuinely embrace because you are passionately devoted to seizing the opportunities it represents.

Most people don't follow their hearts and it drives them crazy, but if you pursue a dream that you're crazy about, you'll thrive no matter what. Even more important, you'll be extraordinarily happy and satisfied with how your life turns out, and that is an exceedingly rare and extremely valuable experience in this world.

HIGHER EDUCATION

A predominance of research confirms that those students who enter college before deciding on a major field of study are the most likely to drop out.[15] They lack the motivation to continue and eventually leave school without completing their studies and earning a degree.

So why is there so much pressure to go directly from high school into college? Some say young adults are already in the frame of mind to study. If they spend time away from school, they risk losing their momentum and not going back, so it is important to stay in school.

But if that were true, why do statistics show that more and more adults do actually return to school long after graduating from high school and entering the work force?[16] Whatever their motivations are for returning, the fact is that many people will go back after a long absence to earn a diploma. Many of these older students are more focused, more interested in the curriculum, and they make better grades than they did when they were younger; they have a better idea of why they are there and what they want from a formal education.

Meanwhile, a high percentage of people who do go to college directly following high school end up working most of their lives in a career that is not related to the degree they earned.[15] Or they enter with one major in mind but switch majors, wasting precious time and tuition because they cannot find a degree program that really captivates their interests. In the worst case scenario, a student will graduate with a major that is less than thrilling to them, but because they have that degree, they settle for a job in that field, even though they don't particularly like it. Therefore, many graduates set their lives up for misery and regret.

I switched my college major four times before graduating with an exercise physiology degree that was useless as far as my career was concerned. I did not know what I wanted to pursue after high school, let alone college, so after several changes I just studied exercise physiology because I liked to work out and wanted to know about muscles and exercise. What I did not know at the time was that there are very few careers for people with that kind of degree, and none of them were jobs I would enjoy doing.

If young adults don't know exactly what they want to pursue as a career or profession, they shouldn't enter college right after completing high school just because that is what is expected of them. Students should go to college only because they want to go and have a passion for higher learning. By the same token, when college is the next logical step to move you closer to your goals, don't hesitate to enroll in college classes immediately.

Everyone's situation, circumstances, and opportunities are different, so decisions about higher education should be made on a case-by-case basis. What is right for one may not be right for others. But don't make decisions based on what your siblings, friends, or even parents want for you. Your decisions have to be based solely on what you want for your own life.

GETTING MARRIED

Similarly, don't get married just because it's the next logical step after dating the same person for a certain length of time. The Centers for Disease Control and Prevention statistics state that the marriage rate in 2009 was 6.8 per 1,000 total population, while the divorce rate was 3.4 per 1,000 total population in the same year.[17] That indicates that about half of all marriages end in divorce. Please don't misunderstand that are we advising against marriage. We are simply stating that if you are thinking about getting married, before you commit to marriage make sure this is the right decision for you and you are not pressured by the "just because syndrome."

We surveyed several divorced people and asked why they chose the person they married. Here are some real-life responses:

"She put up with me, and she's tall."

"He was the only boy to ask me out in high school."

"She had sex with me on the first date."

"I wanted to have a baby."

"He seemed so much nicer than my other boyfriend."

"People thought I was gay."

"He had a cool last name."

"To get my parents off my back."

"I was sick of dating."

"She was hot."

"She was a good cook."

"He made a lot of money."

"Her parents were rich."

Dig deep and explore the honest and authentic reasons why you are getting married. Don't get married just because it seems to be the logical next step or just because you are enchanted by the idea of a wedding ceremony and reception party.

Don't settle for marriage just because he or she is the only person who gives you attention. Too many times I've watched friends get married to the first person who requites them; the marriage usually ends in divorce. It's hard to evaluate something like a marriage relationship when you've never had one. But that's no reason to jump into a commitment without considering what you need and expect from a lifelong partner.

Don't settle on a person just because he or she tolerates your habits and mannerisms when others don't. Eventually those behaviors will wear thin and your spouse will lose patience. Don't marry someone just because he or she is physically attractive, either, because beauty is skin deep and fades. Don't get married just because he or she has money or your friends like him or her, because if your spouse loses that money or you lose those friends, you'll also lose the glue that held the marriage together. And remember not to marry someone for other people's reasons, like to get your parents and family off your back or because that is what society says you should do.

Most people spend more time and energy planning their weddings then they do planning what is important to them in a spouse and relationship.

Keep in mind that even if you are madly in love, still go through the decision-making process before making a life-changing commitment. Actually, if you are getting married because you are in love, that is even more incentive to plan the marriage and set goals carefully. Doing so helps to ensure that you don't become another tragic divorce statistic.

DO WHAT YOU LOVE AND YOU'LL LOVE WHAT YOU DO

Remember that to do something extraordinary, you have to like doing it. That's not a new idea. If you do what you love, you'll never work a day in your life. When you do what you love, it doesn't feel like a job. You look forward to it and it keeps you motivated and fulfilled.

But this concept doesn't apply only to work. To become successful in any kind of pursuit, you have to love it. That's true whether you are a grad student engaged in research, a professional athlete passionate for your sport, a musician who cannot live without playing your instrument, or a writer eager to tell a story. Successful inventors are passionate about their inventions, and successful chefs love to cook—and probably love to eat.

The bottom line is that you need to constantly refer back to your goals to diligently avoid falling into the trap of the "just because syndrome." Don't succumb to living your life just because.

CONVERTING RAW PASSION INTO REALISTIC INCOME

Most people have at least one or two passions, whether those involve volunteer work, a hobby or craft, a profession that appeals to them, or some activity they do for sport or leisure. Finding where your passion lies is a huge discovery, because once you know what you love, it becomes exponentially easier to find a compatible job or career that corresponds to and supports that personal proclivity.

Sadly, most people plod through life without ever devoting any significant time or attention to this process of discovery. This lack of initiative leads to rather aimless and lackluster lives with less than satisfying jobs and plenty of regret.

Invest some effort in a systematic search for your passion, taking advantage of these kinds of opportunities to explore and experiment:

❑ Volunteering or taking a lower paying job is often a great way to try different vocations before you commit to long-term employment.

❑ Taking classes in fields and subjects that intrigue you can open doors of opportunity that lead to enjoyable employment.

❑ Writing down ideas or brainstorming can open your mind to hidden possibilities and otherwise unseen opportunities.

❑ Researching an area of interest will often reveal related occupations and job descriptions you never knew existed.

After identifying your passion, try to apply it in ways that produce income.

Internet Commerce

Starting an online business to sell your services or products is a great way to reach a lot of people. To succeed you'll want to become familiar with web-based programs, e-commerce strategies, and tools and technologies of Internet marketing.

Teaching or Tutoring

If you have a passion for something and enough experience at it, try finding a job where you can share that knowledge with others. Working as a private tutor, trainer, workshop presenter, or adjunct professor, for example, may allow you to teach what you know for income.

Freelancing

A freelancer is self-employed, not committed to one particular employer, and can market and sell his or her services to businesses or individuals without the normal constraints of a traditional job. Freelancers' fees are based on what people are willing to pay and what they think their work is worth. Several freelance websites help connect freelancers with clients. Freelancers do practically every kind of work you can imagine: photography, writing, web design, computer programming event planning, corporate sales, carpentry, interstate truck driving, and more. Pick your passion and freelance it.

Consignment

If you have a product but little or no capital to start a business, you may be able to sell it on consignment. This means that you arrange the sale of your product through an existing outlet. When your product sells, the consignees usually split the profit with you, according to agreed upon terms. They pay for only the items that sell instead of purchasing inventory from you in advance. If it doesn't sell, you can take it back, so it is a low-risk proposition for both you and the outlet.

MISSED OP:
View from the Window

The dreams of my childhood haunt me in my waking hours. When I was young, all I ever wanted to do was ride horses. I'd always loved animals, but especially horses, and on my sixth birthday, my aunt sent me a check for $50 for riding lessons.

A barn across town offered lessons, and I started taking them weekly. The $50 my aunt sent ran out quickly, but my parents were able to cover the cost, at least for a little while. I had four siblings, though, and there never seemed to be enough money. When my mother came to me with the news that they could no longer afford to pay for the lessons, I think I cried the whole night. I lay in bed with tears streaming down my face and hoped that when I woke up the next morning, a horse farm would have magically appeared across the street and I would be free to ride any horse I wanted, whenever I pleased.

The next day my mother drove me to the barn, and I asked my instructor if there were any barn chores I could help out with in exchange for lessons. My instructor smiled and said there were always stalls that needed to be mucked, water buckets that needed to be scrubbed, and horses that needed grooming. And so, I was able to continue my horseback riding lessons into my teen years.

There was no way, though, I'd ever be able to afford my own horse to compete at horse shows at the level I wanted to. My parents were pressuring me to take as many honors classes as I could and spend every spare moment I had studying. Taking a course load of five AP classes left little room for anything else.

"You're a smart girl," my mother would say to me as she stood in the doorway of the room I shared with my sister. I'd be at my desk, surrounded by a mountain of books, my eyes already starting to glaze over from the studying, even though I still had several more hours of it ahead of me. "You're a smart girl," she'd say again, and eye the pile of books on my desk. "And just because your father and I can't afford to send you to college doesn't mean you should miss out on the type of education you deserve. There's a lot of competition nowadays, and you've got to do all that you can to stand out from the crowd."

So I studied, though I still went to the barn once a week, mucked out stalls, helped the younger kids tack up their ponies, and had my lesson. While the other girls that I'd grown up riding with plaited their horses' manes and tails for upcoming shows, I trudged home to hit the books. Summer wasn't any better; I was no longer in school, but I worked forty-plus-hour weeks scooping ice cream, hoping for tips.

By the time I actually made it to college, I'd stopped riding altogether, even though the school I chose had an equestrian team. I would have to try out for it, and I figured there was no way I'd make it, going up against girls who'd owned their own horses since they were five years old. So I studied, got good grades, and eventually decided to major in education and become a teacher.

It was around this time my two older siblings started adding to their families. First, my brother and his wife had a son, and then, three months later, my sister and her husband had twin girls. At family cookouts, people started looking at me, wondering why I wasn't even married yet.

Aaron and I had been dating since my sophomore year of college. He was usually at those cookouts, and one night, on the Fourth of July, after the fireworks, he proposed. I said yes because I couldn't think of a reason to say no.

We bought a home in a semirural area, next to a five-acre parcel of mostly woods. Adam and Eliza were born on our one-year anniversary. Twins, it seemed, ran in our family.

Both Adam and Eliza were what you might call "high needs" babies. They were constantly fussing, fretting, not wanting to be picked up but not wanting to be put down. It seemed I spent most of my days nursing babies, cleaning up after babies, soothing babies.

Throughout it all, though, I found my thoughts drifting back to horseback riding. There was no way I'd be able to do that now, but I hoped perhaps sometime in the future. It might even be something Eliza and I could do together.

It was around the time the twins turned two and were generally easier to deal with that two things happened: I found out I was pregnant again, and the five-acre parcel next to us was sold. I was too busy feeling nauseous and chasing the toddlers around to pay much attention, though. The land was cleared, a foundation was poured, and the house frame was erected. Another building was also being constructed, closer to the eastern edge of the property, so from my window over the kitchen sink I could watch it being built. It seemed too big to be a garage, but it wasn't until it was almost completed, being painted red with white trim, that I realized it was a barn.

At first, I was excited. The twins and I talked about what kind of animals we thought might live in the barn, and we watched as what seemed like miles of post-and-rail fences were built. And then Charlotte was born, and I forgot about the barn for a while.

I don't remember exactly when it was, but I know I was bone tired.

I was at the kitchen sink, washing dishes that had accumulated from breakfast, lunch, and dinner. It was summer and the sun was only just starting to set. My hands seemed to move independently of me; they scrubbed and rinsed and set the dishes in the strainer not because my brain was firing any signals to my muscles but because I'd done this routine so many times I was really just running on autopilot.

But then there was movement outside that caught my eye. I looked up and watched a gleaming chestnut horse break into a trot, then a gallop, and practically fly across one end of the pasture. Its coat caught the sun's rays and appeared to be aglow, as if lit from the inside. In trying to manage life with three children, I'd completely forgotten about the barn next door.

The next morning, though, before my husband dashed off to the insurance company, I asked him if he knew anything about the place. He shrugged, distracted, as he tried to wipe grape jelly from Adam's mouth.

"It's a riding academy?" he said, though it sounded more like a question.

"Can we go pet the chickens?" Eliza asked.

He smiled at her. "I don't think they have any chickens, sweet pea, just horses." And that was it.

Of course, he'd never known about my love for horses; by the time we'd met, it had been years since I'd been on a horse. And I never brought it up because he never asked, not about horses or about what I really loved in life. That seems strange to say it now, that the man I married never once inquired about my passions, just assumed he knew, assumed it was children because I was a teacher, and also assumed I would want plenty of my own.

As summer wound down and the school year was about to start up, I found myself eager to get back to the classroom, to be doing something I was good at. Still, the presence of the horse farm right next door stirred feelings of both joy and regret. There was nothing more soothing—after having been up before dawn, getting kids ready and dropped off at daycare, spending another eight or more hours at the middle school, picking up kids from daycare, rushing home, preparing dinner, and finally, finding myself standing at the kitchen sink—than looking out the window and watching any number of horses frolicking, grazing, kicking up their heels just for the fun of it. But at the same time, as I stood there up to my elbows in hot, soapy water, sponging off plates for the billionth time, the rooms behind me a complete war zone of kids toys, unfolded laundry, and myriad other things I'd meant to throw away and never gotten around to doing, I couldn't help but wonder what my life would be like if I'd made time for horseback riding as I'd made time for all those AP classes. Would it, perhaps, be me building my own barn and owning a dozen beautiful horses, teaching lessons to eager young students, encouraging them to follow their dreams? I rinsed another plate, picked up a handful of silverware. I remembered that night so many years ago when my mom first told me they couldn't afford to pay for my lessons anymore and I fell asleep, dreaming of waking up to a horse farm right across the street, how, at the time, that would've been the best thing in the world.

I told myself that I'd walk next door the first chance I got, sign up for the very next lesson available, but before the thought had even passed, I knew there was no way because there were always children to look after, or a floor to be vacuumed, or a family to be fed. I'd done exactly what was always expected of me, and though it certainly wasn't the worst life, it was a life in which I'd have to be content to watch my dreams from the window above the sink.

WHAT NOT TO DO:
❒ Go along the traditional path of life just because
it is expected of you.

ADVICE:
❒ Follow your passions, even if it means taking a
different path from the one in front of you.

❐ Set achievable goals that lead toward your dreams
   and commit to pursue them.

BOUNDARIES

It may be hard to imagine some people saying that there is nothing else they'd rather be doing than their jobs. After all, how much should we actually like our jobs?

On the one hand, if you overestimate the answer to that question, you might spend your whole lifetime searching for your dream job, even though you've already found one that makes you happy. But on the other hand, if you underestimate the answer, you'll tend to stop searching too early, like most people do, and you'll never be fulfilled. You'll end up settling for work you really can't stand.

So it helps to set some parameters, definitions, or boundaries.

❐ "Do what you love" doesn't mean do what you would like to do every moment of every day. I'm sure even Albert Einstein had moments when he wanted to forget about physics for a while, but he completed the current equation at hand because he had a strong work ethic.

❐ At any given time we may wish to be sipping umbrella drinks in a tropical paradise or sitting down to our favorite meal instead of slogging away at the work in front of us. But that doesn't mean you don't love your job.

❐ The rule about doing what you love assumes that you are fulfilled by the vocation over a certain length of time, not thrilled silly by it every waking second of your existence. Even the most enjoyable pastimes can, at times, fail to live up to our wildest expectations of pleasure.

❐ We aren't suggesting that you do whatever feels good to make you happy in the short-term; rather, we are recommending that you choose a professional career or job that makes you happiest over a sustainable timeframe of weeks, months, and years.

Before accepting a vocation, research which occupations will help you meet your goals while also holding your interest and kindling your passions; then find enjoyable work for the foreseeable future. Sure, you'll have days that are subpar; that's just the way life works in this imperfect universe. But you'll have more days feeling amazed that you are actually getting paid to do something you like so much.

At the other end of the spectrum, set a boundary that helps you like your work and the results it produces more than you like being unproductive or just wasting time in mindless pursuits. The concept of "killing time" should never enter your mind if you are passionate about your life, because you'll always look forward to being actively engaged in rewarding activities. Instead of being tortured by the passage of time, you'll wish you had more than twenty-four hours in a day.

This is not to say, of course, that you should become a workaholic, spending all your waking hours working. You can work only so much before getting tired and losing focus and motivation. Everyone needs a periodic break to unwind, relax, and refocus. Everyone needs a healthy balance between work life and personal life. The idea is to be well-rounded and to enjoy whatever the activity by giving it your full attention. But achieving that state of mind comes from choosing activities you can really put your heart into without resentment, reservation, or regret.

If your work is not enjoyable, you will manifest problems such as procrastination, lack of inspiration, loss of energy, low self-esteem, and even anger or depression. You'll have to force yourself to work, and when you resort to pushing yourself to complete tasks you hate, the results are always distinctly inferior.

Do that kind of dreaded work long enough and you'll unconsciously start to internalize your displeasure in such a way that you will begin to even despise yourself. Self-loathing can turn even the brightest and most gifted individuals into miserly, bitter, hopeless, uncaring, miserable souls.

WELL-MEANING ADVICE AND ALARM BELLS

Although it is easier advice to give than to follow, do not make prestige, social pressure, or even money the main deciding factors when it comes to your career. Examine your interests and skills, and make sure that what you do with your life resonates with you instead of setting off internal panic buttons, alarm bells, and warning sirens.

Prestige and status, for example, can distort your beliefs about what you genuinely want, convincing you to strive not for what you like but for what those around you define as success.

For instance, lots of people try to write novels because they notice that people who write bestsellers win prizes, praise, and fame. What could be more wonderful, they think, than the life of a novelist?

But liking the idea of being a novelist for fame and fortune is not enough; you have to like the work of novel writing. Sitting countless hours in front of a computer screen writing, rewriting, editing, reading, researching, and then revising drafts is just the beginning. To be really good at it, you have to do that for years or even decades, and often accept more criticism than praise along the way. So if you don't actually enjoy the day-to-day process and mechanics of writing, you'll never last long enough to reap any results, much less rewards or accolades.

Money also leads many people astray, but the size of your bank account does not equal the volume of your happiness or contentment. Dollars may be a convenient way for society to measure success, but it's unwise to calculate your personal fulfillment and satisfaction in financial terms alone. Add up all that you value, too, because they may be golden. Unless your life's work is in alignment with your true passion, you run the risk of setting yourself up for disappointment by never achieving your real dreams. One test of whether people love what they do is if they'd do it in their free time without getting paid. Would you do your job for no pay? Your answer will usually be a pretty reliable indication of whether you're in it for the right reasons.

Regardless of what input you get from your advice pool who wish you well and only have your best interest at heart, if you are following your true passion you should have no nagging doubts or lingering questions. Listen for the sirens and alarm bells that go off in your head or heart to warn you when you are heading down the wrong path. If you hear them, just use your trusty goal-planning strategies to reevaluate your decisions and make sure you stay on track and in sync with your personal dreams.

DISCIPLINE

With such powerful forces to lead us astray, it's not surprising we find it hard to discover work that we really enjoy. Most people are taught in childhood to accept the axiom that work equals displeasure. Those who escape this misconception are often very happy successful people.

But a sense of enjoyment often depends on your perspective, so if you're stuck with a job you normally wouldn't enjoy, try to find something about it to like, or make an adjustment that will improve the situation. And don't feel bad if you don't succeed, because all is not lost. The simple fact that you can admit to yourself that you're discontented enough to want to make changes puts you way ahead of the pack, since most people in similar situations will just remain in denial. They'll stay in a job they don't like until they retire, never questioning their circumstances. Listen to your gut. Stick to your goals. Follow your plan with discipline and determination. Eventually you'll find your ideal opportunity.

Some people know what they want to do from the time they are ten years old, and they seem to glide along to their desired destinations. But more often than not, people either follow their careers like the trajectory of a ping-pong ball, or they settle for the first halfway decent job that comes along. Don't throw in the towel so easily. Research your interests. Look for ways to make a living at what you love. You'll follow a much straighter and more rewarding path to success and will achieve enduring satisfaction.

If you enjoy what you do, then being successful at work takes less discipline than people think. When you enjoy your work, it does not feel like work at all, so your job takes on a new and different meaning. The challenge is to find the work you love, and that's where focus and discipline are so important.

One way to cultivate focus and discipline is to always work hard and take pride in whatever it is you do, even if you don't particularly like it. You'll develop the habit of doing things well and not falling into laziness, and that attitude is always a positive asset that opens doors of employment opportunity and career success.

One situation where I always recognize and appreciate workers who have taken real pride in their jobs, even if they don't enjoy it, is when I use a spotlessly clean public restroom. I immediately acknowledge that whoever accepted that task put 100 percent of their effort behind it, elevating a humble, menial job into an outstanding professional display of exceptional work ethic, strong self-esteem, and pride in their work. Such dedication to a job well done, even if it is a thankless endeavor, is impressive. That kind of attitude will always lead to unforeseen opportunities and plenty of invitations to accept greater responsibility with appropriately better compensation.

LET A HIGH SCHOOL KID
DRIVE YOUR BRAND-NEW CAR?

If you had just purchased a brand-new Ferrari, would you hand over the keys to a recently licensed high school kid with no driving experience? Probably not. So why allow a high school kid to get behind the wheel of your entire adult life and determine what direction it will take? You're asking for trouble because the youngster could get lost, take wild detours, get into accidents, or wind up in jail for traffic violations.

Unfortunately we all do just that, for that's the process of life. We transition from childhood to adulthood like a driver going from zero to sixty miles per hour in a blur of acceleration and whiplash speed. We make life-changing decisions while we are still young, inexperienced, and uninformed. As teens, we are led to believe that we have more than enough sense and information to take charge of our choices.

But even if you head off to college or sign up for military service right out of high school, you probably still have little idea what kind of work you are good at or what kind of vocation you'll enjoy. If you're lucky you'll get an internship or two along the way to help you decide which direction to take, but many careers don't offer those. Even the ones that do will often teach you as much about the job as being the batboy teaches you about playing baseball or managing a baseball team.

It takes time and experience to figure out what you want to do for the rest of your life and what you will be passionate about for the long haul. In the overall scheme of things you will get the desired results, however, from honestly following your instincts; making, revising, and sticking to your goals; always gravitating toward what you want to do and really love; and applying yourself 100 percent to every task, project, and job that comes your way. You'll be happier, more productive, and more satisfied . . . and that will open doors to opportunities that you never knew existed.

Since you've consistently and continually outlined your goals, you'll recognize those opportunities when they appear. By capitalizing on each one and seizing it while you have the chance, you will be led step-by-step on an efficient trajectory and pleasurable path toward the realization of all your lifelong goals and dreams.

Adapt, Adjust, Overcome

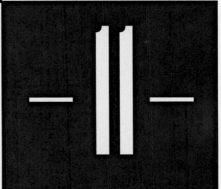

As an opportunity unfolds, it may not play out exactly the way you planned, so it's wise to have a flexible game plan. Remember this motto: Prepare by staying aware.

You can only adapt to changing circumstances as they arise if you have spotted them in time, so don't get complacent. Stay vigilant. Familiarize yourself with the forces at work and study your available options. Analyze the ins and outs of every possible scenario you can imagine. Then pick the best one as your contingency or "Plan B."

Don't hesitate to alter various aspects of your original plan if that's what it takes to overcome obstacles and emerge victorious. Those who are too rigid in their thinking are usually too inflexible in their doing, and agility is the name of the game when it comes to capitalizing on rapidly evolving opportunities.

As Yogi Berra famously said, "It ain't over 'til it's over." Plenty of lopsided games suddenly shift direction when those who become overconfident take their seemingly imminent victory for granted. Lots of apparent winners lose at the buzzer or right before crossing the finish line, and many champions emerge victorious in the fourth quarter, the last inning, the final lap, or the final seconds of the very last round.

EMBRACE CHANGE

Much of the stress we experience in life is due to an inability to accept change. Most people are so set in their ways that change throws them off kilter, but the truth is that the only absolutely predictable fact of life is that change happens.

After a major change, we go through a transitional phase during which we attempt to cope, adjust, and gain new bearings. Depending on the significance of the change and the mind-set of individuals experiencing it, the transition can last anywhere from a few minutes to several decades, and during that period they will likely feel uprooted, confused, and stressed. But if we respond to change in a healthy, proactive, appropriate manner, these transitions become opportunities for knowledge, insight, compassion, resilience, and success.

People usually cope with change in stages, much as they cope with grief or regret. How long each stage lasts, and the order in which the stages come, depends on the individual and varies from person to person.

Oftentimes the initial reaction to change is fear. There is certainly nothing wrong with feeling fearful because that is, after all, nature's warning mechanism. Fear awakens our senses to a heightened state of alert and forces us to pay attention.

Practice controlling your response to fear so that it does not inspire panic and prevent you from taking appropriate action. One tool for overcoming the paralysis that fear can cause is to practice dealing with it in mock scenarios, the same way you might train your family members to evacuate the house in case of a fire.

The more you prepare for worst-case scenarios, the less likely they will startle you, because you have already confronted them in your training. For example, imagine fearful circumstances related to the opportunity you are trying to capitalize on, and then troubleshoot to come up with common-sense or effective solutions.

Another stage of change is resistance. Resisting change is common because humans become acclimated to their situations and lifestyles, and once they get cozy, they don't want to step beyond the familiar comfort zone. In fact, this tendency is so great that people who may not even like their situations are often still quite resistant to changing it. We see this in inmates who do not want to be released from prison; they would rather sacrifice becoming a free citizen than face the challenge of change.

Don't resist change; this natural phenomenon occurs every day to all of us. Embrace it as part of the process of being alive, and flow with your circumstances, even if they are not what you had anticipated.

Usually compliance or acceptance eventually follows any negative feeling that may have arisen from experiencing change. If a change is not going away, make the best of it. Adapt, adjust, and overcome any obstacle it brings with it.

When change becomes part of your normal routine, it is easy to accept its presence because you don't need for it to go away to move forward. For those of us who want to become more comfortable with change, we practice embracing it by taking baby steps. Sitting in a different seat in school, shopping at a different grocery store, or driving a different way to and from work are all examples of how we can practice getting used to small changes in our lives. Those may seem like minor exercises, but by implementing rather insignificant changes, we accustom ourselves to a lifestyle that invites change. We no longer resist it, fear it, or get perplexed by its sudden onset; instead, we learn to negotiate transitions and navigate changing environments without losing our way or getting distracted from our main focus.

Three Tips for Dealing with Change

1. Expect It: Changes will happen, be they good, bad, or indifferent. Be open to them, and accept them as part of the process in seizing opportunities to enjoy the rewards of success.
2. Stay Positive: Remember that every change or obstacle you face opens a door to opportunity. With a positive attitude, expect the best and then go for it with focus and enthusiasm.
3. You've Rehearsed for It: Everyone has coped successfully with changes at one point or another. You've survived changes. Think of those changes as dress rehearsals for this new challenge

No matter what form changes take, every one of them brings another chance for a fresh opportunity. Do not fear or resist change, but embrace it as a transformative event that will bring you new skills and experience and help propel you forward toward the attainment of your lifelong goals and dreams.

Change is the essence of life.
Be willing to surrender what you are
for what you could become.

Unknown

ADAPT

Cockroaches are believed to be the oldest group of insects on the planet, which indicates how successful they have been at adapting to change. One reason for their success and endurance is that they have learned how to eat many different foods. Most creatures stick to one type of food and when that source runs low or disappears, the species is starved into extinction. But not cockroaches! They just move to a different section of the buffet.

For humans, being able to adapt is a process whereby one becomes better suited to new surroundings and learns to succeed. When people realized that their food supplies dwindled in winter, they not only learned to grow food or raise livestock for meat but also to preserve food and store it for later consumption. If our ancestors did not succeed in their adaptation, the human race would not have survived. Humans had to evolve to deal with changes in climate, famines, predators, and diseases.

Example of adapting can be seen all around us. During their training exercises, Navy SEALs sometimes hike through knee-deep snow in Alaska and then strip off their layers of insulated clothing, jump into a partially frozen lake, and tread water. Indigenous people living in deserts get used to walking barefoot over scorching hot sand, and high-rise construction workers learn to enjoy a picnic lunch while balancing on skinny steel beams thirty stories in the air.

Humans are capable of this kind of extreme activity because over time we can adjust to harsh or strange environments, both mentally and physically. In the same way, as we practice mental flexibility in the pursuit of opportunities, we also learn to adapt and to change. This experience and evolution helps us survive failures or setbacks.

When faced with an opportunity, if we do not adapt we will not be in the most advantageous position to succeed. So adaptation is an essential skill for anyone who wishes to lead a successful life. If you try to control every situation and fight back against your environment, you will be engaged in a losing battle, because nobody can control events around them for a sustainable period of time.

People who have exceptional adaptive traits are able to generate creative, constructive, positive actions, no matter what unexpected circumstances they face. Think of adaptive behaviors as skills that allow us to be flexible when change occurs, and follow these tips to hone your adaptability:

1. Stop and think. Thoroughly analyze and research the situation. View actions and consequences from different perspectives.

2. Consider your lifelong goals. Ask yourself, "How does this help or hurt my opportunity to achieve my lifelong goals?" or "How might this choice affect my life, job, family, friends, and future?"

3. Be prepared. Constantly increase your knowledge and skills through formal or self-taught education. Practice your adaptation exercises. Refer to your goals and tweak and refine them. Change happens to everyone. If you are ready to handle it, you will embrace the new opportunities it brings into your life.

4. Don't see problems, just new opportunities for solving them: Every problem or challenging situation is a chance to open the door to new opportunities and increase your knowledge and expertise. Even circumstances that seem most devastating carry within them seeds of new knowledge and experience. So don't see difficulties only as problems; rather, see challenges and obstacles as rare chances to try out new solutions that will help you prove your adaptability and eventually come out on top.

The reasonable man adapts himself to the world;
the unreasonable one persists in trying to adapt
the world to himself.

George Bernard Shaw

ADJUST

Most people do not embrace change; they resist it. It is human nature to become comfortable in the accustomed way of doing things, so any change will at first feel uncomfortable for most people. Naturally, they react by trying to avoid it. On the other hand, successful people with agile minds embrace change so much that they are constantly looking for it. They like to do those uncomfortable things that most people won't, because they know how rewarding the outcome can be. With opportunity comes change, so if we cannot adjust to that change, we make ourselves incapable of welcoming opportunity. When most people see change coming, they see a red flag, which scares them off, but successful people see a checkered flag waving them closer to the finish line and the winner's circle.

Nothing unfolds exactly as planned; obstacles and roadblocks always get in our way. Those tend to be more daunting as the opportunities get better, too, because the stakes are higher, which usually means the path is less traveled and more difficult.

Meanwhile, adjusting to change brings unique challenges. We are haunted by what-if scenarios and doubts, and we second-guess the situation every step of the way. We can easily overanalyze or think too deeply, though, overcompensating in a way that creates even more problems. Rather than thinking too hard in a way that grows into worrying and fretting, it is often best to prepare (Ready), take focus (Aim), make your move and get busy doing (Fire!).

Start small. When making an adjustment to your game plan, it may turn out that all you need is that tiny little tweak, so taking things in manageable increments can help you avoid unnecessary major changes.

If those small changes do not get you where you'd like to be, then larger adjustments may be required. But by doing things in stages, you develop your mental flexibility, confidence, and courage along the way, and the whole process becomes easier.

Fast and Severe

When pursuing an opportunity you may, however, have to make fast and severe adjustments. If you were driving your car down an empty road and a large boulder fell from above, you would have to slam on the brakes and jerk the wheel to the left or right. That's not an ideal way to drive, but it's required in an emergency. The same thing sometimes happens in life when we are pursuing an opportunity. So be prepared for a fast, abrupt, severe change.

Slow and Gradual

Over time, slow and gradual adjustments may also be needed to succeed. The same example of driving can be used. If you were driving on a long straight road and saw an obstacle in the distance, you would slow down and approach it slowly or move over to another lane to avoid it. In either case, slow and gradual adjustments were made over time to avoid the distant obstacle.

Multidimensional

Even more common than fast and severe or slow and gradual adjustments while capitalizing on opportunities are multiple adjustments. Some obstacles will come at you fast, even as you see others looming on the distant horizon.

A better approach is to prepare yourself before adjustments are required. Start building courage and developing essential skills before you are forced to. Bruce Lee had a lightning fast ability to block unexpected incoming kicks because he had practiced doing that thousands of times in preparation. From an early age he ate a particular diet, hung out with a certain crowd, followed a specific routine every day, and set goals. To bystanders the result seemed like a superhuman feat or a miracle. But really it was just the dramatic and sensational final expression of success at the moment of impact when he seized the opportunity for which he had diligently, intentionally, and patiently prepared.

Wise and prudent men . . . have long known that in a changing world worthy institutions can be conserved only by adjusting them to the changing time.

Franklin D. Roosevelt

OVERCOME

Obstacles and adversities are found in all aspects of life, and when you are working through an opportunity they may be more prevalent . . . and also more vital to your success. How we adapt, adjust, and, most important, overcome what is put in our way will define our futures. Without struggle there would be no victory, just as without rain there are no rainbows. Without overcoming adversity, the feeling of success would be dulled and diminished. Overcoming adversity by using our minds and bodies to persevere and push past our fears builds character. With strong character, the obstacles get weaker and easier to vanquish.

Henry Ford said that life is a series of experiences, and each one makes us bigger, even though sometimes it is hard to realize while it's happening to us. He said that the world was built to develop character, and we must learn that the setbacks and grief we endure help us move onward.

Adversity is unavoidable. But throughout this book we have outlined and explained skills and techniques to prepare for it. By practicing positive skills and learning techniques, you will develop the right mind-set of internal fortitude, which will empower you to overcome any problem or adversity life throws your way.

Making mistakes is inevitable and unavoidable, but suffering after making them is entirely optional because you have the power to control how you react to events. Even under the worst circumstances, you can choose to focus on the positive and use it as a learning experience, rather than focusing on the negative and suffering feelings of regret.

In the latter part of the nineteenth century, Washington Roebling was appointed lead engineer to build the Brooklyn Bridge. A couple of months after receiving this assignment, an incident left Roebling with permanent brain damage. His body was paralyzed, rendering him unable to speak. But he taught himself to communicate by tapping on his wife's arm like Morse code. For the next ten years he tapped on his wife's arm, relaying all the critical instructions about how to complete the bridge. Today the Brooklyn Bridge is one of the main arteries for the most important city on earth, and it stands as an enduring symbol of Washington Roebling's ability to adapt and overcome insurmountable problems in the passionate pursuit of his dream.

When faced with adversity:

❒ Be optimistic. Redefine the problem or obstacle as a new opportunity to solve your way to success. If you confront a locked door, don't turn away; it might be a vault full of gold for the taking. Find the right key or combination.

❒ Stay determined. Push through fears, slide on past negative people, and sidestep obstacles. Give yourself credit and a pat on the back for every little success as you continue to win small battles on the way to a major victory.

❒ Break down problems. Any huge problem can be solved if you divide it down into manageable steps. A massive jigsaw puzzle looks impossible to solve, but even a child can do it by taking it one piece at a time in child-sized problem portions.

❒ Try multiple solutions. An explorer tried to light his matches, but they were wet from snow. So he used a slice of ice to make a crude magnifying glass. With that to focus the rays of the sun he started a fire. Investigate all possible options before deciding on a course of action or giving up on success.

❒ Stay focused! Don't let an obstacle derail your plans for success. If a wall is in your way tunnel under it. Build a ladder over it. Hike around it. Add three more walls to transform it into a brand-new building. Stay on track.

❒ Stay motivated! Read motivating books and listen to inspiring audiobooks. Constantly remind yourself of the stories of how successful people overcame challenges.

We have learned that the adversity we face does not predetermine our fixed position in life, even if unequal opportunity or misfortune blocks our paths. It is our attitudes and actions to overcome challenges that ultimately define who we are and where we go in life. We have to cultivate the attitude of a warrior, stand firm, and not let negative thoughts rule us.

During my career in law enforcement, I learned many lessons I value to this day. But none were more essential than those I learned about adapting, adjusting, and overcoming adversity. During much of the training we were instructed that if we did not adapt, adjust, and overcome adverse situations, our lives would be at risk. Whether it was dangerous undercover work, the arrest of a violent criminal, or a raid on a drug lab possibly rigged with explosives, we quickly learned to think on our feet and rely on our keen preparation.

If you want to succeed in any area, consider these principles of adapting, adjusting, and overcoming adversity so valuable and useful that your life depends on them.

During an undercover operation, I was blindfolded and led into a dark room. Through the blindfold I detected flashing strobe lights; loud music was blaring, which disrupted my thoughts and disoriented me. I had no weapon and was surrounded by multiple hostile drug dealers. I was supposed to negotiate a drug transaction and then leave the premises with a date and time.

I wore a transmitter, but it was not working, so my backup lost what apartment I entered. Adapting, adjusting, and overcoming to this evolving dangerous situation became a necessity to escape with my life.

As soon as I entered the room, the hood was jerked off my head and I was tackled from behind by one guy, as another one screamed questions at me about who I was working for, and a third guy shouted that I was going to be killed. I had to quickly adapt to my surroundings by blocking out the loud music and voices, surveying the room for an escape route, searching for an improvised weapon, and keeping track of the number of hostiles and their positions in the room. I had to make rapid adjustments to my original plan because negotiating a drug deal was suddenly out of the question. My new goal was to survive. Going for my weapon was not an option, since I had none, and between me and the door were three large men trying to restrain me.

In my mind I had to create a plan and then physically execute it to overcome the situation at hand. The first objective was to get to my feet. I tried several times and kept getting knocked back down. Finally, I saw a new opportunity to escape when one thug turned his back to me. I grabbed one of his arms and pulled him to the floor, kicking away another one as I bolted for the door. Knocking two down and pushing one out of the way, I made it out of the room successfully, constantly evaluating and reevaluating my circumstances and adapting to new obstacles with extreme flexibility and focus during a whirlwind of spontaneous action.

The ability to quickly adapt, adjust, and overcome, combined with determination and hard work, were the skills I needed to open that door and take advantage of the opportunity to escape with my life. The lessons learned that day still serve me well in all facets of my life.

That was an extreme and dramatic situation. But the point is adaptability is a trait that will help you succeed against any number of threats, obstacles, adversaries, or adversities. Remember, experience is the best teacher, even if it is someone else's.

Think of important opportunities as life-changing or life-threatening situations that require decisions made quickly and efficiently. You don't know when or if you will ever see that opportunity again, so it may very well be your once-in-a-lifetime chance to reach your dream.

The greater the obstacle, the more glory in overcoming it.

Moliere

MISSED OP:
Helping Hand

The first time I had seen him in over four years was on the television set one lazy Sunday afternoon as I was flipping through the channels. The older of my two sons had already moved out and gone to college, having just graduated high school a few months before. My youngest was at a friend's house for the day, and Dan, my husband, was outside doing yard work. I was changing channels relatively fast, and if I had blinked, I would have missed it.

Actually, that's not necessarily true. No one could have missed that jet-black hair and those sharp, piercing blue eyes after having seen them in person.

"... twenty-five-year-old Kevin Mullin is currently in the custody of the local police department after several eyewitnesses reported seeing Mullin fire his gun at another man, allegedly a fellow member of his gang. His victim, eighteen-year-old Jason Lambeth, was reported dead on arrival of the hospital, after taking the gunshot to the head."

"Oh my God," I said under my breath. I sat on the couch for a long time, gripping the remote control as if it were my saving grace before letting it clatter onto the coffee table. I ran through the screen door to my husband.

I first saw Jason Lambeth when he was twelve years old. He was in the sixth grade with my oldest son, Lance, and they were assigned to work on their class science project together. I remember Lance asking me if it they could work on the project at our house. "I asked him if we could go to his house, but he said it wasn't a good idea. His mom sleeps a lot and doesn't like having company."

I told him, yes, of course, his classmates and friends were always welcome at our house, although I thought it was odd that the little boy had said his mom sleeps a lot, but I shrugged it off as the slightly inaccurate description that often comes out of a twelve-year-old's perspective.

Jason arrived at our home on his bike later that afternoon. I immediately decided that he was the most adorable kid I had ever seen, next to my own children, of course. His jet-black hair was cut in the short, textured cut a lot of the young boys wore at that time, with little unruly spikes throughout. He was a skinny, knobby-kneed kid with a slightly pointed nose and bright blue eyes.

I introduced myself to Jason and told him if there was anything they needed to just let me know, although they were working on a volcano project and I was not the right person to ask about science. Dan, however, picked up the slack for me. He spent the entire afternoon on the back porch with those boys, while I stayed inside tending to my four-year-old and watching them out the window. When it got to be late afternoon, I began preparing a large plate of finger sandwiches and cookies to take outside to the boys.

"Would you boys like to stop and take a break for a snack?" I asked as I stepped outside to join them. My question was immediately answered as both boys dove at the plate. Lance took two small sandwiches and a cookie, while Jason wolfed the majority of the plate's contents. It was as if he hadn't eaten anything decent in weeks.

I couldn't help but laugh. "Are you hungry, Jason?" I joked.

"Heck, yes! This is the first thing I've had to eat all day!"

That caught me off guard. "Really?"

Jason shrugged. "My mom doesn't like to cook or fix things to eat. Usually I eat peanut butter out of the jar or something."

"What about lunch at school?"

"I usually pack my own lunch, but if we don't have anything for me to take around the house, I just kind of eat off my friends' plates. They don't mind."

Yeah!" my son chimed in. "I always let him share with me; it's no big deal."

This entire conversation made me very sad and a little sick to my stomach with anger, wondering what kind of mother doesn't do the very basic parenting responsibility of feeding her child.

The boys worked until it began to get dark then decided to call it a night. Jason told Lance good-bye, got on his bike, and headed down the driveway. I ran after him.

"Jason, wait! It's dark outside, sweetie. Why don't you come inside and call your mom to come pick you up?"

"Nah, it's okay. Even if she does answer the phone, she's probably not going to want to come get me. It's okay, I only live over on Taft Street."

"Taft Street?" I repeated. That was all the way on the other side of town. You had to drive under an overpass to get to it. "No, I don't think so, buddy. Get in the car, your bike will fit. I'll drive you home."

Jason obliged, not that he had a choice in the matter as far as I was concerned, and we drove the seventeen-minute car ride across town to his home. Taft Street wasn't in the best part of town; most of the houses were run-down, and it seemed like the part of town that housed all the drug addicts and prostitutes. I reminded myself that it's not right to judge in that way.

"Which house is yours, sweetie?" I asked.

"Oh, it's the white one up here."

I looked around until I saw a white house. "You mean . . . the one with the bright flashing lights?"

They were indeed the lights of two police cars.

"What the—" Jason flung open the car door and ran toward the house. "Mom? Mom!"

I got out of the car and followed him. I noticed a woman around my age, mid-thirties or so, being lead out of the house in handcuffs. I approached an officer.

"What is going on here?" I asked.

"Are you family, ma'am?"

"No, but that boy is a friend of my son's."

"Well, I'm afraid his mother is going to be locked up for a very long time. This is her third strike and she is being charged with prostitution and buying and selling heroin.

"What about Jason?" I asked, suddenly a lot more worried.

The police officer shrugged. "He doesn't have any other family. No relatives and no known father. He's going to have to go into foster care."

"No, don't do that. He can come home with me."

"Are you a state registered foster parent?"

"Well, no . . ."

"Then no can do; social services will have to place him in a home."

I opened my mouth to argue, but decided against it. I gave Jason one more look, and our eyes met. His eyes seemed to plead with me. I lifted my hand in a wave, got back into my car, and drove away. On the way home, I decided, rather impulsively, that I wanted to adopt that boy if his mother would let us.

"I think we should adopt him," I told Dan that night as we got into bed. "I know it sounds crazy, but I really think that he needs a stable family. His mother is going to be in prison for at least ten years, and I don't want to see him bouncing around from one foster home to the other."

Dan sighed. "He is a nice kid, but don't you think this is a little irrational? We just met him today."

"Yes, I know, but, I don't know. I feel strongly about it. He needs somebody like us, I think."

"I think our own children need us first. We don't know what kind of risk we are taking letting this child into our home. With the kind of background he is coming from, this could be asking for trouble. What if he tries to harm one of our own boys, or what if he is just a horrible influence on them? Do you really think it's smart to commit to that kind of risk?"

I closed my eyes and rubbed my temples. "You're right, that makes sense. I just didn't get that impression about him."

"I tell you what," Dan said, reaching out to hold me. "Let's sleep on it and pray about it. Let's not make any decisions tonight while we are so tired."

"Okay," I agreed.

I didn't get a good night's rest. I tossed and turned throughout the night, thinking about my husband's rational words versus my own feelings. I eventually fell asleep sometime late in the night and woke the next morning with what I thought was a clear head. I gave my husband a kiss.

"I think we should continue to pray for him, but I think you're right. It's not worth the risk to our own children."

"I thought about it through the night, too," Dan replied. "I started to think it might be the right thing for us to do, but I think you are right, as well. It's not something we should do."

And that was that.

Over the next couple of years, I saw Jason around from time to time. He was placed in a foster home in our area, and was able to stay in the same school and stay friends with Lance. He came over a lot, and the boys would play video games or toss a ball around in the backyard. I never again brought up the idea I had that night, nor did Dan, although I believe we were both still thinking about it. I also started to notice that Jason was changing in some negative ways, but I couldn't put my finger on what exactly it was.

We began to see less and less of Jason, and when the boys got into high school, we didn't see him at all. I think the last time I saw him was when he was fourteen and playing football in our backyard. One day when Lance was in the tenth grade, I asked him if he still went to his school.

"Yeah, he's still around. I mean, when he actually comes to school, that is. He skips a lot. I think he hangs out with some older guys."

"Oh, I see," I responded quietly. "Is he still in foster homes?"

"Yeah, I think so. Not the same ones, though. He gets moved around a lot, but they keep him in this area so he can go to the same school, which is pretty cool."

Two years after that conversation, just about three months ago, at Lance's high school graduation, I waited for Jason's name to be called.

It never was.

"Dan! Dan!!" I ran outside where my husband was doing yard work, with tears streaming down my face.

"We should have adopted him! We should have, but we were too scared! And now he's dead! He's dead; he's dead. He is dead!" I sobbed.

Dan stopped in his tracks. "You don't mean that Jason boy, do you?"

"Yes, Jason. He was killed by a fellow gang member. He never had anyone who loved him enough to keep him out of gangs and out of that kind of trouble. He's dead now." I was on my knees now, sobbing into the grass.

"We could have adopted him. We could have helped him in so many other ways. Why didn't we? We might have saved his life."

In my eyes, it wasn't the gunman who was responsible for his death. It was me.

Now I have to live the rest of my days with the regret of not helping that young boy when I had the chance.

WHAT NOT TO DO:
❑ Make a decision at an emotional time and not revisit it.

ADVICE:
❑ Weigh the positives and negatives of a situation
   before making a decision.
❑ You may have to adapt, adjust, and overcome
   obstacles when faced with an opportunity.

Mastering Failure and Rejection

-12-

Everyone has been rejected and everyone has tasted failure at one time or another. If you meet a person who says otherwise, they are either lying or delusional—or they haven't experienced life in the real world.

But before we move into a discussion of how to defeat or control fear of rejection and failure, we must first clearly understand what the two terms mean and how the two experiences or feelings are related.

You may be saying to yourself, "Who doesn't know the meaning of rejection and failure?" You're right; I agree with you there. In most cases rejection and failure really don't need explaining. But it is important to learn how they overlap and intertwine, and to do that we have to examine each of them separately and in a little more detail and depth.

Rejection is essentially turning down a request. Rejection is related to the word ejection, which means to throw out, in other words, a dismissal. You want to join a club or borrow money, but your application is rejected. Your poem gets rejected by a magazine because the editor doesn't like it, or your advances are rejected by the person you have a crush on.

Failure, on the other hand, is the condition of not meeting an intended objective. You cannot do enough pushups, so you fail the tryout for the gymnastics team. You try to contact an old high school friend, but since they moved away with no forwarding address, you fail in your attempt. When you went on the roller coaster it wasn't scary enough so it failed to live up to your expectations of a thrill ride.

Because rejection and failure are closely interrelated, rejection will always carry with it a sense of failure, and if you fail at something, you will likewise come away with a feeling of rejection. You cannot feel one without the other. For example, since that particular roller coaster failed to excite you, you reject it as one ride you'll never again take. But that doesn't mean that all roller coasters are boring or that you should never again spend money on amusement park rides.

Let's examine another more common example of failure and rejection that almost everyone has experienced at one time or another.

John sees an attractive woman sitting at the bar and decides he wants to date her, but first he has to strike up a conversation. He strolls over, sweaty palms and all, and introduces himself. But she cuts him off mid-sentence. "Sorry, not interested."

John has been rejected, but he also feels the sting of failure. He has no way of knowing whether his particular attempt to start a conversation failed, or whether she would have rejected anyone who approached her. But like most fellows, he assumes that he failed because of something he did or did not do, and thanks to his own personal failure, he also got rejected.

In this way rejection and failure almost always overlap. They leave people like John doubting themselves and their abilities, and along with that loss of confidence comes a fear of future rejection and failure. All of this undermines self-confidence, and when people move into this downward spiral, they can lose their courage, determination, and optimism. That's why many people never even attempt to reach their goals or fulfill presented opportunities. They dread the prospect of having to go through the potential embarrassment and humiliation of rejection and failure.

If you are like most people, you have been conditioned to view rejection and failure negatively and to always take it personally. So every time what you do fails or is rejected, feelings of worthlessness and insecurity are reinforced. That is one of the most common problems people face, and it's nothing to be ashamed of because we've all been there and done that. But if you are able to overcome those negative feelings by not letting yourself be vulnerable or susceptible to that kind of perceived rejection and failure, it will do wonders to empower you.

Believe it or not, success is not limited by failure or by rejection. What hurts our chances for success is the fear we feel. Many wildly successful people have pasts that are littered with failures and rejections. What distinguishes them, however, is that they are not scared of failing or getting rejected. So they keep trying, and eventually they win.

Consider the facts:

❐ John knew nothing about the woman he approached. When she said she was not interested, it may not have been because John failed to live up to her standards. Her not talking to him may not have been a rejection at all.

❐ Maybe she was just in a sour mood or had just experienced a bad confrontation, so she acted rudely. Maybe she just came from a funeral and wanted to be left alone to drink in silence.

❐ What if she were an undercover cop working a case? Maybe she needed to be left alone to keep an eye on her suspect.

❐ She could have been an actress who used the experience with John at the bar to practice a part, so that when she went to her audition she could reject the guy in the screenplay and make it look real and convincing.

The point is there are a million and one reasons why her telling John to basically get lost may have had nothing to do with John. So his perceived failure and rejection may have been just a big illusion dreamed up in John's own head.

He could have had great success in approaching the next beautiful woman who walked into the bar. John will never know, however, because after not succeeding in his first attempt, he developed a powerful fear that kept him from trying again. From John's limited perspective, it felt like he failed, and because he failed, he was rejected. He walked away thinking, "I'm not good enough." To protect himself from that kind of unpleasant experience in the future, he learned to be afraid. Now because he is afraid of rejection, he is definitely a failure at meeting new women in bars because he is scared to even talk to them. His fear of rejection created a self-fulfilling prophecy of failure.

Teachers told Thomas Edison he was "too stupid" to learn anything, but it didn't destroy his confidence to succeed. Donald Trump went bankrupt, but it didn't squelch his enthusiasm to keep trying to get filthy rich. By all accounts Abe Lincoln was a rather unattractive-looking guy. But he didn't get scared of being rejected because he wasn't handsome. He maintained his sense of strong self-identity, and now a beautiful and flattering statue of him is in the nation's capitol.

Fear of rejection is a learned response that we are taught when growing up, and it stems from being trained and conditioned that those who are rejected are pushed out of mainstream society.

Fear of failure is drilled into us the same way, because we are conditioned to think that if a person fails, he or she isn't worthy or wanted, because we want winners, not losers.

But the real losers are those who reject themselves. If you cannot accept yourself for who you are, no matter how successful, loved, admired, talented, or fantastic you are, it won't make you satisfied or happy. That's a tragic failure of the worst kind.

Fear of failure and rejection is an energy-robbing state of mind that leads to self-defeat, self-destruction, and emotional paralysis. This kind of fear encourages irrational thinking and behavior, resulting in a personal lack of confidence that ultimately hinders the ability to take action when faced with an opportunity. As Mr. Spock from Star Trek would say, "The fear of failure and rejection is an irrational one."

Think about it. If you are rejected, what did you lose? Nothing! You are still in the same situation you were before the rejection. Maybe you didn't gain anything, but nothing was taken away from you, either.

Before John walked over to the pretty woman, he did not know her nor did he have a relationship with her. After John was rejected, he returned to his seat, completely whole and intact. He still didn't know the woman and still was not in a relationship with her. He was right back to square one.

What did John lose? Some people may say he lost pride or confidence. But that was not snatched away from him by failure or rejection. He brought that loss on all by himself.

If John had been trained and conditioned to use that rejection as motivation to move on, he wouldn't feel a loss of pride or confidence. He would just accept that sometimes our opportunities do not pan out exactly the way we hoped or planned.

In most other cases, if you take a risk and fail or get rejected, you might not lose anything at all, but you may gain valuable experience. Even when failing there can be a great lesson that will help you seize your next opportunity at success. So don't be afraid to take some risks.

Above all, don't consider yourself a failure or a reject just because one of your plans failed or got rejected. You're still worthy, valued, capable, and deserving of success.

DON'T DWELL ON FEAR

How does fear affect opportunity? The fear of rejection and failure stops us from taking chances or taking that next step toward opportunity. The fear of rejection is debilitating and can prevent or delay an action or decision. Past experiences that left us fearful of rejection or failure may put us in a more defensive state of mind, and that will hinder the ability to take advantage of future opportunities.

Unfortunately, that kind of fear has reached epidemic proportions in modern society, and fear is the driving force that keeps millions of people from being all they can be and all they want to be.

But many times it is just the timing of our actions that determines whether or not we are successful at grasping an opportunity. An author once put it very accurately when describing the difference between a successful gunfighter and one who loses the duel and dies. "It's not who draws his gun the fastest that counts, it's the one who aims and pulls the trigger first that makes all the difference." When an opportunity presents itself, be ready to take action without hesitation and follow through with it completely.

Even the slightest tinge of fear can slow us down or create irrational doubts just when we need to think and act fast, so controlling fears often facilitates the mastery of goals.

Fear of failure and rejection can handicap our confidence and abilities, while a single attempt to achieve a goal will often lead to many other unknown opportunities and chances for success.

Fear is the path to the dark side. Fear leads to anger.
Anger leads to hate. Hate leads to suffering.

Yoda

If you let the fear of failure prevent you from following your dreams, you will never succeed. The more you let that fear dictate your thoughts and actions, the more it will consume you and the more you will be afraid of life and of all its myriad possibilities. Let go of all your preconceptions and disentangle yourself from those experiences that frightened you in the past so that they don't make you scared to embrace the future.

Volumes of books are devoted to the subject of overcoming fear and insecurity. But there are some easy ways to help you start the process of neutralizing or overcoming your fear of failure and rejection.

MISSED OP:
Losing Las Vegas

Tony Anderson grew up in a big house near Boston. He loved spending time with his parents, brothers, and friends. His grandparents lived right down the street. It was a close-knit family and community.

When he was young, Tony didn't really have a care in the world; however, when he was ten years old his dad, a local policeman, was shot while making a routine traffic stop. Even as an adult, Tony still remembered hearing his mom get the call like it was yesterday.

"Hello. He's what?! Oh no! Where is he? We'll be right there!" She broke into tears and hung up the phone.

Within six months his dad had recovered fully and was back on the job, but it was a rough six months. Tony was named after his dad and had always looked up to him, but he found himself looking at his dad with a newfound respect and admiration after that incident. He wanted to become a police officer, just like his dad.

Several years later, Tony sat in a classroom taking the written police exam for the Las Vegas Metropolitan Police Department. The LVMPD was recruiting new officers from all over the country. Tony was picked to fly to Las Vegas and continue with more tests and interviews for the job. After a successful first round, he made it to the next stage. He flew to Las Vegas three more times over the next couple of months. He was well on his way to becoming a police officer in Las Vegas.

It was on one of those trips to Las Vegas that Tony realized a lot of real estate was for sale in Las Vegas. At about $50,000 per half acre, the real estate prices were low, too. As Tony walked by one particular lot, he said to himself, "I wish I could buy this property and move out here. I bet I'd make a bundle on real estate!"

Tony loved the scenery and activity of Las Vegas, too. He'd never seen anything like it. Tony thought he was really needed as a police officer in Las Vegas.

During the third long flight home from Las Vegas, Tony was watching an in-flight movie when the plane hit some turbulence and the passenger next to him began to panic. She was a young girl traveling home from college for the holidays and she didn't have much experience with flying.

"Calm down. It's only turbulence," Tony said.

"I can't help it! I'm not used to flying!" said Sandy.

"We'll be there soon."

"I just want to see my family again. I want to tell them how much I missed them!" Sandy replied, as the plane began its decent to the airport.

In that instant, Tony thought about his own family. How would he feel being separated from them if he were to live clear across the county? Then he thought about his close friends. Could he really handle seeing them only a few times a year? Thoughts of being in a new environment all by himself started to take over and fear set in.

All of those thoughts flew through Tony's head as the plane landed at Logan Airport in Boston on that chilly December night. Then, when he got down to baggage claim and saw his entire family waiting there to greet him, he made up his mind. He was going to pass on the Las Vegas police officer job.

"I'm so glad to see you!" Tony replied, as he embraced his whole family.

A few years passed and Tony got married and bought the house he'd grown up in. He had landed a job as a security guard at a local bank. He had never bothered investing in Boston area real estate, though. It was too expensive and Tony had never had much money.

On their fifth wedding anniversary, Tony's wife, Samantha, had a surprise for him.

"How would you like to go on a gambling trip to Las Vegas? I've been saving up for it for a while now."

Tony thought that the trip was a fabulous idea. When they got there, however, Tony didn't want to gamble right away. He wanted to go to that little spot just off the strip where he'd seen that vacant lot years before.

He was sad, but not at all surprised, to see that the vacant lot was now a huge casino-hotel. Tony looked up at it for a good ten minutes before shaking his head and slowly walking away.

He was going to go drown his sorrows at the gaming tables in a different casino when he noticed a police officer walking down the sidewalk toward him. For just a moment, Tony envisioned himself as that officer and the life he could have had if only he hadn't let his fears control him.

WHAT NOT TO DO:

❒ Let fear control your actions and decision making.

ADVICE:

❒ Know that achieving something means you might have to take some risks.

❒ Use fear as energy to stay focused and motivate you through uncomfortable situations that lead to your goals.

AVOID EXCESSIVE REVISING

While in school taking multiple-choice tests, the teacher would advise us that our first answer was usually the right one. If we had doubts and changed the original answer, we increased our chances of getting it wrong. Sometimes we have a tendency to spend so much time and energy revising what we've done that we can't get anything else accomplished in the meantime.

Overthinking can yield diminishing returns. For example, the more times you revisit a topic after putting in the adequate amount of effort to research it, the more you run the risk of getting bogged down in an overload of too much information.

There is certainly nothing wrong with revisiting a project, and in some situations it may be valuable. But sometimes it is more effective just to finish what you've started, consider it done, and move on to something new. Making a firm decision and sticking to it is often far more useful and will propel you forward much faster than sitting and pondering all the many possibilities. In real-life situations there may be no opportunity to go back to the original script, so beware of becoming too dependent on the revision process.

SUCCESS REWARDS THOSE
WHO RISK REJECTION AND FAILURE

If you don't play your hand, you will never win, even if you are holding a royal flush. It is better to be a "has been" than a "never was," because at least the "has been" made an attempt to accomplish what he set out to do and gained knowledge and experience that will help him succeed next time around.

Thirty-eight publishers rejected the novel Gone with the Wind by Margaret Mitchell until finally Harold Latham of Macmillan published it. Author Stephen King received dozens of rejections for his first novel, Carrie. One publisher told him, "We are not interested in this kind of science fiction because it does not sell." King is now one of the best-selling authors of the modern era. Authors Jack Canfield and Mark Victor Hansen were rejected 140 times before their blockbuster Chicken Soup for the Soul was accepted for publication. These iconic American writers took many risks and faced much rejection before becoming ultra-successful on the heels of seeming failure.

Art critics rejected Vincent van Gogh in his day, but recently one of his pieces fetched the highest amount of money ever paid for a painting. The Jimi Hendrix Experience band was booed off stage during one of its first tours of the United States, and a high school prom dance committee in Tennessee refused to let a young Elvis Presley play at their dance because they thought he lacked talent. Howard Stern was fired from his first big radio job for not abiding by the rules, but now he is one of the highest paid talk show hosts in radio history. Kids in her school ostracized Marilyn Monroe because they said she looked too plain to ever be popular.

You may have to pass through 10, 100, or 1,000 rejections before getting the acceptance you seek, but keep in mind that life often bestows the greatest success on those who persevere.

TURN REJECTION INTO MOTIVATION

The most important piece of advice in this book may be this simple statement: "Let failure fuel success and turn rejection into motivation."

Whenever I feel my motivation waning, the most effective way for me to get it stoked again is to close my eyes and briefly think back on all the rejections and failures of the past. Pondering like this allows the experience of powerful feelings. Each of us is different, and some will feel anger or rage. Others will sense sadness, despair, or regret. But feelings produce energy. Let that energy flow through you; then take all of that emotional intensity and convert it into positive momentum. Think of those past failures as stepping stones to get you to a place of success.

The best revenge is massive success.

Frank Sinatra

FAIL FORWARD

We wrote Missed Ops to help you reduce the probability of failures by learning from the experiences of others, but that doesn't mean you will never fail. Even the most successful people in the world experience failure.

Abraham Lincoln failed in business in 1831. He was defeated when running for the legislature in '32 and again failed in business in '34. His sweetheart died in '35, and he had a nervous breakdown in '36. He lost another election in '38 and was defeated in his run for Congress in '43, again in '46, and once more in '48. He ran for a senate seat in '55 and lost, so he tried again in '58 but was again unsuccessful. In between those two failures, he ran for vice president in '56 and once again tasted defeat. Four years later he ran for the highest office in the nation and became the 16th president of the United States.

Abraham Lincoln was, in the eyes of many historians and Americans, the most successful president we've ever had.

If he could continue to persevere despite so much adversity and emerge victorious after repeated failures, so can you.

Most people view failure as the apocalypse, the end of the world. They regret their circumstances and dwell on the disappointment, which only handicaps them with a negative attitude. But successful people look at failure from a completely different perspective. Perception is the key, and a successful person interprets failure as positive feedback and a valuable learning experience.

To learn anything, you must risk failure, and the experience of actually failing is the fastest way to learn. After a failure occurs, debrief by asking yourself what can be learned from the experience to lead you to triumph next time.

Professional athletes figured that out a long time ago, which is why players, coaches, and trainers have been relying for decades on videotapes of lost games, matches, or performances to help them win championships. Football coaches "study the tapes," playing back their failures and reviewing them to find out what went wrong so that they can revise their plays and strategies. Golfers analyze their golf swings with the help of slow motion video and then tweak their stances or grips to improve performance and accuracy. Boxers study the rounds of each match until they find an opportunity to exploit or take advantage of a split-second opening and score a decisive knockout. They know from experience that failure will tell them exactly what to do, and what not to do, to win.

So as soon as a failure transpires, write down what happened so you can do a kind of post-game analysis and make a diagnosis. Realize that the only time you've really failed is when you fail to learn from your mistakes.

MISSED OP:
Making the Cut

Football. That was the sport to play when I was growing up. All my friends were on teams in the peewee league during our elementary school years; and I would have been, too, if my parents would have let me. But football was too dangerous to their way of thinking. They wanted me to play something safer, like baseball or soccer; something that didn't involve being knocked to the ground by someone bigger than me.

So, I didn't play football like my friends. I tried my hand at the other sports, but they just didn't have the same appeal. I wanted to play football! I wanted to wear a helmet and shoulder pads. I wanted to carry the pigskin down the field, not bounce balls off my head or run around bases. My parents were adamant, though. Football was out of the question.

They tried to redirect my interests by enrolling me in other activities. They tried guitar lessons, swimming, even karate, but none of it interested me. I attended my friends' games as often as I could, and I followed the NFL teams on television faithfully. I wanted the one thing I was told I couldn't have.

When I entered ninth grade, I finally saw my chance. Tryouts for the high school football team were taking place. I forged my parent's signature on the permission slip and showed up on the field at the appointed time. I would finally get to play football!

But showing up for tryouts, I found out, doesn't guarantee a place on the team. I was not prepared for the drills we were expected to perform. All the other guys trying out had been playing football for years. They knew the routine. They came prepared. I didn't even have the right shoes or gear. I didn't understand the commands being shouted at us. I was lost.

Besides floundering through the drills, nothing in my overall physique or performance set me apart from the other guys. All that the coaches saw was a kid of average build with zero experience in the game. They crossed me off the list. I didn't make the cut.

I watched as my friends and peers made the team, while I was sent home. My first opportunity to fulfill my dreams and I'd blown it. I'd never been more devastated in my life. I determined right then and there that next time I'd be ready. And I threw myself into pursuing my goal.

I started by reading and researching physical training. I wanted to make sure that the coaches would notice me, that they would see a well-built athlete not just an average teenager. I spent my entire freshman year studying and strategizing how to turn my body into a mean, lean football machine.

During my sophomore year, I put my plan into action. I began working out with weights to build body mass. I began running to improve my endurance and speed. At the same time, I also began studying the game that I had loved for so long. I hung out with my friends who were on the team and gleaned as much as I could from their conversations. When tryouts came around for my senior year, I knew I'd be ready.

Finally, the time arrived. It was tryout time. My friends encouraged me to sign up and tryout. But I hesitated. Was I really ready? What if I failed to make the cut, just like I had two years before? The thought of going through that kind of disappointment again, especially after working so hard for two full years to prepare, was horrifying. I couldn't do it. The fear of failure paralyzed me into inaction. The week for tryouts came and went, and I let the opportunity pass me by. My friends may have had confidence in my success, but all I saw in the mirror was the scared little freshman who was not good enough.

I was disappointed in myself for not trying out, but I buoyed my spirits by setting my sights on a new goal: college football. After all, college level ball would have even more prestige than high school. With another whole year to prepare, I was sure to make the college team. I put the missed tryouts behind me, began focusing on the goal ahead, and continued my training.

Tryouts for the college team came and went. Each year I put it off, not quite confident of my abilities, and still remembering the feelings of humiliation that followed my failure that first year of high school. I continued to train, continued to study the strategies of the game, but never had the courage to walk back out on the field in front of the coaches. I let each opportunity pass me by, telling myself that I just wasn't quite ready.

Faster than I expected, graduation came, and my college years were over. My degree in exercise physiology and knowledge of football earned me an internship with a college professor who was conducting a study on the athletic training of football players. We measured body fat percentage, sprint times, muscle strength, vertical and horizontal leaping, and the limits of aerobic abilities.

The whole process was fascinating, and I often wondered where I would fit into the ranks of these athletes. I felt that I was as physically fit, but I'd never allowed myself to be truly tested against others. One day, I unexpectedly got the chance to find out.

The professor informed our study group that morning that we all would be asked to go through the same athletic testing that the football players had. The exercise was meant to give us a sense of the kinesthetic perspective of the participants. Knowing that I was in top physical condition, I was excited for the opportunity.

When the day came for our run-through, I pushed myself to reach my highest potential. I knew I'd done well, but I wasn't quite prepared for the results the professor showed me.

My scores were the highest in the group. More shocking than that, however, was that some of my scores were even better than the athletes we tested. I scored on par or better than national-class athletes, many of whom would be going into the NFL and other professional sports. I was speechless.

You would think that I would have been elated to learn how well my training had paid off, but I wasn't. Yes, I was in great condition and quite capable of competing with the athletes I so admired, but it was too late. I'd missed my opportunity, more than once.

My fear of failure, that seed that had been planted in that first football tryout, had developed into a stranglehold on my life. I had let it rob me of my self-confidence and keep me from obtaining my dreams—dreams that were well within my reach.

The regret that came from facing this truth seemed almost as devastating as that failure so many years before. Without realizing it, by trying to avoid failure, I had actually, avoided success.

WHAT NOT TO DO:
❒ Let fear or past experiences of failure control your actions and decisions.

ADVICE:
❒ Achieving something means you might have to take some risks, even facing your biggest fears.
❒ Stay focused on your larger objectives after completing smaller ones.

PERSIST

Motivation is essential to exhibit persistence. Persistence is refusing to relent, even in the face of opposition or apparent impending defeat. Those who persist muster the ability to maintain positive action despite the powerful temptation to quit.

Motivation is the catalyst for that kind of persistence and the psychological or emotional spark that ignites it. There are two kinds of motivation: intrinsic, emanating from within; or extrinsic, coming from something outside.

❒ Intrinsic motivation is typically driven by a passion or enjoyment of the task or process itself, or by a burning internal desire. A self-challenge pushes you onward, no matter what others may think or how the external odds might be stacked against you.

❏ Extrinsic motivation comes from outside, like the carrot dangled in front of the donkey. Rewards like money, good grades, praise, fame, and public adoration often serve as powerful extrinsic motivators.

Although everyone is inspired by extrinsic motivation, most successful people derive their primary drive and inspiration from intrinsic motivation, or what many describe as "heart." Even in the absence of some kind of external reward or recognition, they still have the burning incentive to persist in the pursuit of their goals.

When most people take on a project or set a goal, their motivation will surge at times with lots of high peaks followed by smaller ones. Motivation will come and go; it is difficult to stay motivated for sustained periods of time. That is why, as stated earlier, it is important to set smaller goals that consistently lead to and reinforce your larger ones. Achieving them gives you small rewards along the way, which motivates you to keep pursuing your greater objective.

Keep in mind that motivation does not actually produce tangible results. Results come from action and activity. That's an important distinction, because if you are persistent you can continue to take positive action toward your goal even if you do not feel motivated to do so.

Motivation may set you into motion, for example, which is why the words motive, motor, and motion are derived from the same Latin root movere, "to move." After you get underway, however, motivation might fade or wane. But if you are proactive, you can keep accomplishing results. Achieving results will, in turn, motivate you more. In that way you keep getting closer to your next objective.

If you have ever driven a car you've already experienced a cycle of events, whether you were aware of it or not. When you switch on the ignition, the car battery provides enough juice (motivation) to crank the engine. Then you head down the road. But the battery doesn't have enough power to run all the electrical gadgets on your vehicle and keep the engine firing the entire time you're driving. It would quickly drain its power, and you'd have to constantly replace car batteries the way you do flashlight batteries. Instead, the car has an on-board electricity generation system powered by the alternator, which is a kind of electromagnet. After you start your car, this gadget kicks in, produces electricity to refresh the supply your battery lost when you cranked the engine, and then continues to produce electricity while you drive. After you turn off the engine, however, the alternator stops. To start back up again, you must rely on your battery.

So motivation is the battery that gets us into action, and after we start the journey toward our goals or destinations, the rewarding process or short-term goal attainment keeps rejuvenating our desires. Like the car's alternator, those incremental rewards become our on-board motivation generator to keep the cycle going. We may need to stop along the way, however, and each time we want to get cranked back up again we need our trusted battery: motivation.

The battery doesn't get us from our homes to the grocery store and then to the lake for a holiday picnic, though, it just aids in the process. Action is what gets us where we're going by turning the key, firing the pistons, engaging the gears, and making the wheels roll. Without action a whole garage full of batteries won't get us out of the driveway, and without acting on motivation, we won't accomplish any of our goals. But action feeds motivation, just as our motivation pushes us into action.

My family used to tell me stories of a distant relative who traveled from overseas to the United States to participate in the famous 1849 gold rush. As the story goes, he borrowed a lot of money to come to America and purchase a claim of land where he could mine for gold. But after more than a year with no results and a mountain of debt to repay, he sold his claim for a pittance and cut his losses.

The person who purchased the land subsequently hired a mining engineer who discovered that my distant relative had stopped digging just two feet short of a huge vein of gold. Had he persisted for a few more minutes and shoveled a little deeper, he would have struck it rich.

The story may or may not be true. Perhaps my family just told it to teach their kids about the value of persistent motivation coupled with unwavering action. True or false, the story did remind me to keep going, even when I wanted to quit.

Persistence is pivotal in keeping you moving in the right direction, and the value of persistence comes from visualizing your future. Seeing your rewards and dreams compels you to push on in the face of adversity. Being specific about every vivid detail of what you want in life will allow you to develop a never-quit attitude and automatically become more persistent in your actions and successful in your endeavors.

I use a small line from a not-so-great Rocky movie to remind me of persistence. In Rocky V, Rocky is in a street fight with his boxing protégé behind the local tavern. After being knocked down time after time, Rocky is seemingly out of the fight. As his young protégé turns to walk away, thinking the contest is over, Rocky staggers to his feet and yells, "I didn't hear no bell!"

If you want to reach a goal or snag an opportunity, then run, crawl, or drag yourself forward until it's yours. Don't stop fighting until you hear the bell.

Nothing in the world can take the place of persistence. Talent will not; nothing is more common than unsuccessful men with talent. Genius will not; unrewarded genius is almost a proverb. Education will not; the world is full of educated derelicts. Persistence and determination alone are omnipotent. The slogan press on has solved and always will solve the problems of the human race.

John Calvin Coolidge

Go BIG or Go Home

-13-

While uncovering or creating new opportunities, go big. Look for the major life-changing ones first. Striving for the most rewarding and powerful opportunities will usually automatically open doors to smaller ones that you may not have otherwise recognized. Aim as high as possible, because even if you fall a bit short, you'll still hit an elevated target.

If you are seeking knowledge, strive to learn from the most informed and intelligent people. When benefiting from the experiences of others, strive to find people who have the most breadth and depth of experience. Ask for their help or advice, and if you cannot get that, research to find out more about them, their formulas for success, and their approaches to life and problem solving.

You won't achieve anything by not taking action toward your goals and dreams. Don't sit and watch others chase their dreams while yours suffer from neglect. Get moving and do it now. Take action by outlining your goals. Plan big and visualize bigger! See yourself doing or having something extraordinary; then create a plan to get from where you are now to where you want to be. When dreaming, don't limit yourself or settle for anything less than the best. Don't be afraid to create goals and dreams that are gigantic and lofty, even if they may not seem realistic, because at least then you have set the bar so high that whatever you accomplish will be phenomenal.

Don't make a lifetime goal of being a millionaire when you can just as easily strive to be a billionaire. When you think you can do only ten pushups, push yourself to do 100. If you start counting to 100 and make it to only twelve, at least you achieved something better than you thought you could; whereas, if you set a goal of ten, you are more likely to be content at just eight or nine.

If people tell you you're crazy for dreaming so large, turn that negative chatter into motivation to push harder and prove that they were crazy for not believing in you.

Actively pursue every goal or dream, because you will uncover other great opportunities connected to your original objective. You'll also stumble upon opportunities that may have nothing to do with your goals at that time, but may hold value for you later.

Put your dreams in a one-gallon jar and they'll be less than one-gallon dreams. But give them an entire ocean and they'll grow large enough to float ships, islands, and continents. Throw a kernel of corn into a flower pot and you'll be lucky to get an ear or two, but cultivate that kernel across open, fertile land and you might find yourself with acres and acres of stalks and boxcars full of corn. Plenty of American pioneers we cannot name planted an apple tree in their yards. But Johnny Appleseed planted apple trees across the yards of an entire nation; his name lives on in perpetuity as part of our national heritage.

Think small and ordinary and you'll get a mediocre result. But dream as big as the sky and you give your life an opportunity to expand in a way that fills up that enormous dream space.

MISSED OP:
The World Wide Web

Greg sat in Robert's room, waiting out 1991. Both were seniors in high school and preoccupied—Greg with getting a used car and Robert with his early model Commodore computer. The rectangular box wasn't much to look at, but it was the only computer in the neighborhood, and that gave it a kind of mystic appeal. To Greg, it seemed completely incomprehensible; he thought it better to stick with looking for cars; its finite number of parts and purposes were curious thoughts. Robert, however, with his high IQ, saw the computer with a more familiar eye; to him, it was less like an idol of an alien religion and more like a difficult but solvable puzzle. Much to his parents' dismay, he'd taken it apart and put it back together several times. The intricate maze of wires had always suggested to him that one could do more than just play Miss Pac-Man.

Recently, it appeared Robert had been proven right. He'd spent weeks and months downloading Dungeons & Dragons stories, blocky, pixilated images, and other information from some anonymous source in California, more than 1,500 miles away.

Greg, standing over his friend's shoulder throughout all this, asked several times, "What is this stuff? How did you get it?" He was bewildered by the idea of transferring data through telephone lines.

Robert explained the process to his friend as best he could, but even to his ears it sounded incredible. The struggle to fold such an outlandish concept into his perception of the small, gray box outweighed the immediate benefits. Greg soon lost interest.

Unlike his friend, Robert was intrigued by the challenge. The processor was slow and sometimes unreliable, but it delivered magical results. He imagined the whirring and beeping noises opened the door to a wider world beneath his fingertips. Unfortunately, in addition to possessing remarkable intelligence and a strong, intuitive grasp on the technology behind the system that allowed him to download information, he was also nearsighted, or maybe just lazy. It doesn't really matter; the results were the same. Both boys failed to realize what they had in front of them.

Of course, what Robert and Greg were participating in was the infant version of the World Wide Web, which would go public in two years, completely revolutionizing every facet of modern life. They didn't recognize the magnitude of the opportunity that was staring them in the face. They could have been pioneers in the biggest technological advancement of the twentieth century. They could have been some of the first people to make a career, living, or fortune from the Internet. They could have made one of the first social websites or a directory for buying cars, computers, or even shoelaces. Being one of the first to do anything on the Internet would have yielded amazing results. They could have capitalized on virtually any aspect of what is online today with an almost guaranteed positive outcome.

In retrospect, we readers can easily mentally reprimand these young adults who lacked neither intelligence nor imagination, two qualities people so often use to justify success.

The teenagers fell prey to two common problems: lack of vision in Greg's case; lack of motivation in Robert's. Despite the near-miraculous powers of the World Wide Web, there is still no way to travel back in time and get that second chance; what then, to do?

Nothing, except take the stinging pain of an opportunity lost and use it as a reminder to be aware, not only of what is around you, but also of what is in front of you, anticipate what might happen in the future, and then take action to ensure that you are a part of that future.

WHAT NOT TO DO:
❐ Be close minded or oblivious to opportunities placed
   in front of you.

ADVICE:
❐ Look what is around you, opportunities are everywhere.
❐ Have vision: Look at trends, technologies in the past and
   compare them to a trend on the verge.
❐ Be proactive, act instead of observing.

WARRIOR MENTALITY

Think of what qualities epitomize the perfect warrior. He or she must be resilient, fierce, and strong; able to transform fear into energy and gain tremendous power from adversity while never giving up the fight. Cultivate a warrior mentality while you visualize this internal source of positive determination and inspiration to help you to succeed whenever opportunities present themselves to you.

Once you have developed that warrior image and experienced that kind of empowering mind-set, you can flip it on like a switch whenever things get tough.

TAKE ADVANTAGE OF OPPORTUNITY

Opportunities are the doorways to success. Recognize or create opportunities around you and implement an efficient decision-making process to take advantage of them. Use other people's experience as a guide for what not to do when faced with an opportunity in order to increase the likelihood of success.

When listening to advice, understand where that information is coming from. If you want what they have, then follow in their footsteps; if you want something different, choose a different path.

Create lifetime goals and a plan to achieve them. Record and revisit them often. Working toward your goals will uncover and create opportunities that otherwise would not have been discovered. After your plan is laid out, take action.

To be successful don't forget to work harder than most. Become the hardest worker you can be. Practice hardworking skills and techniques and never quit or surrender. Compete to outdo yourself. But remember that hard work is just one tool in a toolbox.

Plenty of people work hard like mules but never attain their dreams. If you are to achieve big things, focus all of that hard work like a laser beam. Maintain an overall mental picture of your long-range, intermediate, and short-term objectives all at once, but concentrate and drill down on just one at a time, the one right in front of you.

Trying to accomplish too many things at once only dilutes your energy. To walk a mile you do not take 3,500 steps all at once, you put one foot in front of the other, one step, then you repeat the process until you've gone a few feet, several hundred yards, and finally the whole mile. Keep your destination in sight, otherwise you might walk in the wrong direction, but remember to reach one goal before setting off to accomplish the next one.

Don't get stuck in a treadmill routine and lose track of time, either, because life will pass you by before you know it. If you get sucked into a daily grind, you will find it difficult just to survive, much less dream big and stay in hot pursuit of those dreams. Learn new and extraordinary things, practice skills that will make you successful, and strengthen your positive habits. Make sure that your daily routine is based on your unique goals and heartfelt dreams, not just the status quo of the lemmings who meekly conform to today's rat-race civilization.

Someone will accomplish those things you dream about, so why not be that someone? Remember, no one is born into greatness. If you give 100 percent to practicing skills or habits, you will become successful at mastering them, and that will, in turn, lead to big opportunities down the road and a mastery of your major goals.

But you have only a limited amount of time each day to pursue your dreams, so invest your time wisely and prioritize your actions. Carving out an hour here and a few minutes there enables you to make gigantic gains, so don't be complacent, remain vigilant.

It is easy to derail major goals and dreams if you don't stick to an overall game plan and strategy. With big opportunity comes the potential for even bigger mistakes. Carefully weigh the risks and rewards before making major decisions, because one error can compound into another, triggering an avalanche of mistakes. Avoid trouble. Gravitate toward positive situations. Keep the company of positive people. And if you do make a big mistake, accept it; then regroup and formulate a new strategy to get you back on track.

Do not settle for less in life! Build your self-confidence and mental attitude to expect the best, believing that you deserve it, whether you're dreaming of wealth, health, family, career, or anything else you desire. If you don't like the direction that some aspect of your life is heading, change it. Others may say that you are supposed to be a certain way or fit into a particular mold, but that's not true. You have the power to shape and design your life any way you want in pursuit of the very best this world has to offer.

Change happens always and everywhere, and the key to achieving extraordinary things is to embrace it. Look for changes to usher in new opportunities, and be flexible when dealing with evolving circumstances. Adapt, adjust, and overcome obstacles. Successful people don't let change dictate their attitudes and trajectory. They use the momentum of change to propel them out of their present circumstances and forward into a better life.

Master failure and rejection and you have taken a rare step toward becoming an exceptionally successful person. Use the feelings triggered by rejection and failure as a motivator. Each rejection and each failure makes you stronger and smarter as its builds character. Those challenges toughen up your mental fortitude, so embrace the lessons you harvest from failure and rejection.

Develop a warrior's mentality of never giving up and never surrendering to failure and rejection, and always get back up on your feet and move closer to the fulfillment of your dreams. If you can't stand, crawl; but don't ever quit!

Engage in every act of your life as if it is your last and you will never be disappointed by any outcome. Remember that the most powerful weapon at your disposal is the human will, and that success belongs to the person who wants it the most.

Force yourself to dig deep inside and give everything you have. And if you do, your life will give you back everything you've dreamed could be yours. Accomplish that and you will never regret any Missed Op.

More Missed Ops

—14—

MISSED OP:
Bitter Son

A tear rolls all the way down my cheek and plunges off the edge of my chin, hitting the leg of my trousers. I don't feel it, of course, but I see the dark, wet circle it leaves. I grip the wheels of my chair for support as I stare into the caskets at the lifeless faces of my mother and father during their wake. After eighty-five years of life and sixty-six years of marriage, they died of natural causes just eight hours apart in their nursing home. Their story has been recorded in the local newspaper as a "Real-Life Love Story." If only they knew that not all of their lives have been a romantic love story. Instead, my parents spent years and years hoping, to no avail, that their only son would call home to say, "I'm sorry," or "I love you."

I was only eight when the accident happened, and being fifty-five now it's hard for me to remember a time when I could walk. I remember only bits and pieces of my pre-accident life: playing ball in the park with Andrew Broussard and the other boys in the neighborhood, climbing the tree behind our house, and, of course, the day I ran out in the middle of the road and got hit by a car. That's the last time I ever remember using my legs, because that's the day they stopped working.

Being a boy in a wheelchair in the 1960s was a lot different from how it is now. There wasn't as much tolerance back then, nor was there a push for "equal opportunity." The boys in my neighborhood, whom I had always considered my friends, started acting like my wheelchair was a disease they might catch, so they kept their distance. The teacher I had at school the year I returned from the hospital treated me like my brain didn't work either. During recess, I sat on the edge of the playground in my chair while all the pretty girls teased me and called me names. I came home crying everyday.

My mom couldn't handle seeing me go through this, so she pulled me out of school. She said I would never have to go back there, and instead she would homeschool me; she would teach me everything I needed to know. She couldn't protect me from getting paralyzed, so she decided the day she pulled me out of school that she would protect me from everything else in her power, particularly emotional harm. Looking back, I believe that was the day in which it all went downhill.

"Mom? Mom?! MOM!!"Five years after my accident, I shouted frantically for my mother from the family room, where I sat in my chair watching a program on the television.

My mother rushed into the room. "What is it, pumpkin?"

"I always have my lunch at this time! I'm used to eating at this time and I'm hungry! Why are you doing this to me?"

Acting this way wasn't out of character. I knew I was perfectly capable of making my own lunch. After all, my arms worked perfectly fine, but my mom never made me do it on my own. After a while I started to believe in my head that I wasn't capable of doing anything for myself.

"I'm sorry, pumpkin. I was cleaning and lost track of time. I'll go make you your lunch now."

"Well, hurry! I'm starving!"

I think I remember this day so well because, before my mom left to go back into the kitchen, she held her gaze on me for longer than usual. There was a distinct look of hurt in her eyes. I could have sworn I saw her eyes start to gloss over with welling tears before she walked away.

This may have hurt my heart for a moment, but only briefly, for when I looked back at the television, I saw two boys about my age running across the screen with their strong legs, and the anger returned.

Three years later, I sat outside on the porch while my father worked under the hood of his truck. Andrew Broussard, the young man who lived across the street from me for years, jogged over to our yard.

My father looked up from the hood of his car, clearly surprised. He approached Andrew before I could speak. "Can I help you, son?"

"Oh, I just came to talk to Freddie is all."

Dad stared him down for a minute or two, glanced at me, and then returned to his work under the hood.

He looked down at the ground and shifted from one foot to the other. "So, how's it going?"

I shrugged in cold silence.

Andrew shoved his hands into his pockets. "I came by because . . . I mean . . . I know you don't get out much, and . . . well . . . the fair is in town this weekend . . . I thought you might want to come with us."

I started at him for a minute. This was the first time in nine years that he, or any of the neighborhood boys, had so much as talked to me, let alone invited me to go anywhere with them.

"The fair grounds are just a few blocks away. We were going to walk—I mean . . . you know . . . get there without using our cars. It should be fun."

I'm not sure what came over me at that instant; maybe it was desperation to get away from my parents for once, or maybe it was that I knew it would worry Mom and Dad out of their minds if I went. For some cruel reason that thought thrilled me.

"Sure, fine, I guess I'll go." I shrugged.

"Awesome!" Andrew said. "Meet me at my yard at seven and we'll head over there."

"Okay." I acted nonchalantly, but inside I was more excited than I had been in years.

Of course, that night, I got in a fight with Mom and Dad, who didn't think I should go.

"How are you even going to get there?" She paced and wrung her hands. She couldn't keep the panic out of her voice.

"It's down the road, Mom. The guys are walking and I can roll my chair!"

"Oh, that's just great. How are you going to roll your chair all the way down there when you need me to help you out of bed and wheel you to the breakfast table?"

"I don't need you to do anything! You do it for me because you think I'm an invalid! It's just my legs that don't work; the rest of me works just fine!"

"Don't talk to your mother with that tone!" Dad roared at me. "She waits on you hand and foot, day in and day out, and you have the nerve to disrespect her like that? If you're so capable of taking care of yourself, then maybe you should do something for yourself for a change, instead of hollering for your mother to be at your beck and call!"

"Fine, maybe I will! But I'm going to that fair tonight."

I wheeled out of the house and rolled my chair over the lawn and across the street. I looked back into the kitchen window and saw my mother fall into my father's arms, sobbing. I knew she would be worried about me all night, but I didn't care.

In that one night, I snapped at a girl who offered to help push my chair across a particularly muddy part of the field and made her cry, I demanded that someone go buy me a lemonade and then snatched it out of his hand when he brought it to me, spilling some lemonade on a different girl's shoe, and I managed to offend everyone in the group that night with my constant brash talk. I finally just went home early.

Andrew never came over and invited me anywhere else after that, nor did he ever talk to me again.

I woke up on the morning of my twenty-sixth birthday in the same bedroom I grew up in, and bitterly reflected on my life. I never graduated high school or went to college. I never got a job or got married, and I never left my parents' house.

In that moment, I decided it was all their fault. My mother pulled me out of school in the third grade. It didn't matter that she did it to protect me. I was still living here at age twenty-six and I had missed a lot of opportunities to make a better life for myself because of my parents' decisions.

That evening, my mother showed me the beautiful cake she had made for me for my birthday. In response I violently knocked the cake off the table. It hit the ground with a splat. My mother threw her hands over her mouth and gasped. My father was speechless.

"I hate you!" I screamed. "I hate both of you! You ruined my life! Just because I am in a wheelchair doesn't mean that I couldn't have had a successful life and you have done nothing but try to take that from me!"

"I'm sorry. I didn't mean to. I only wanted to protect you! I just wanted you to be happy!" My mother said through tears.

"Well, you failed. I'm miserable. I hate my life, and I hate you!"

That was the last night I saw or talked to my parents. I stormed out of the house that evening, wheeled to the highway, and hitchhiked ten hours away. The rest is history for me, but for my parents that was the night that life stopped. After they found out where I was, they wrote letter after letter apologizing. I never responded to any of them. I was too bitter, too angry, and too full of hate to care that without my correspondence or apology, my parents would spend the rest of their lives grieving the loss of their only child.

It's not until now, after all these years, as I sit by my parents' corpses that I realize they were never the problem—I was. I was angry with myself for running into the street in front of the car that hit me that day. I was bitter with myself for allowing my parents to treat me as an invalid all those years. They were overprotective, but they weren't unreasonable. They didn't stop me from going to the fair that night, and they wouldn't have stopped me from going back to school and getting my education if that's what I really wanted. But I didn't do those things, because I preferred to wallow in self-pity and allow my disability to rule my life.

To this day, I've never made a decent salary, I live in a small apartment, and I've never been married.

I reached inside the casket and held my mother's cold, stiff hand, the same hand that had, at one time, pushed my wheelchair from the bedroom to the breakfast table and labored over a birthday cake that I threw on the floor.

"I'm sorry, Mom. I'm sorry to both of you. I shouldn't have said I hated you that day. I love you both. Thank you for everything."

But of course, they couldn't hear me. They couldn't give me a hug and tell me that they forgive me. I had waited too long, and it was too late.

I sat there next to their bodies and cried into my hands, thinking that missing the opportunity to tell my parents how sorry I am feels like losing my legs all over again.

WHAT NOT TO DO:
❏ Dwell on the past. Let regret, anger, bitterness, or fear change you for the worse.

ADVICE:
❏ If an unforeseen circumstance arises, use it as motivation to achieve your goals.
❏ Adapt and adjust to overcome any obstacles in your way.
❏ Persevere in spite of roadblocks.

MISSED OP:
Bonnie Wasted Time

Bonnie had dated John since they were sophomores in high school. When Bonnie was nineteen, John asked her to be his wife. She was insecure and scared. She knew she wasn't ready for marriage, but she couldn't stand the idea of not being with John. So she reluctantly agreed to marry her high school sweetheart.

About a year later her infatuation with John began to fade. As they both matured, they grew apart and felt more like roommates then husband and wife. Three years into the marriage Bonnie made up her mind to leave John, and the choice made her feel liberated and free. Bonnie felt bad that her decision would hurt John, however, so she postponed doing anything about it for another year. Twelve months later Bonnie mustered up the courage and told John she wanted a divorce. John was upset and told her to wait another year. Bonnie stayed with him for another two years. Things never got better, but Bonnie did get pregnant.

She thought maybe having a child would fix their problems and they would be the happy family she always envisioned. But shortly after the baby was born, the feelings of unhappiness returned. She stuck it out for another two years. Bonnie wanted to leave, but now she couldn't afford to be on her own while taking care of a child.

Bonnie saved up for three years so she could move out and get a place for herself and her child. Finally she got her divorce and left the man she had not loved for the past decade. She wasted much of her young life in a marriage almost entirely devoid of love. Her twenties were gone, and she was a single mother setting out on her own for the first time. If only she had expressed her true feelings in the first place, she wouldn't have wasted ten good years in the prime of her life. She loved her child, but she could have been raising a family with someone she really loved had she followed her heart from the beginning.

WHAT NOT TO DO:
  ❐ Take time for granted.

ADVICE:
  ❐ Take action
  ❐ Seek help or advice from others who have
    had the same experiences.

MISSED OP:
Follow Your Passions

Those who love us want what is best for us. But parents typically base their guidance and recommendations on their lives, not ours. They may be able to point us toward the destination, but we have to take our own journeys, even if that means following a route less traveled because we find it more interesting and exciting on a personal or career level.

During my second year at a local community college, while working toward a Criminal Justice degree, my grades began to suffer. As a supportive solution, my mother generously agreed to help pay my expenses if I would quit my part-time job at the local deli and fully concentrate on my studies. I reluctantly agreed, but two weeks later I felt guilty about it—like I was living on handouts. So I determined to come up with another way to keep my grades up while also earning money. I was highly motivated and energized by emotion, not just by parental advice and support.

I knew a lot about health and fitness because that was my passion. So a buddy and I took a three-day course and became certified as personal trainers. Within just a few weeks we were running ads in upscale newspapers and magazines. The customers were flocking to us. Personal fitness was a new trend in those days, and it was a big status symbol to have your own personal trainer, which made mine a really high-demand job.

Soon I was making between $1,000 and $1,500 a week in cash, working fewer than three hours a day, and controlling my own schedule as an eighteen-year-old entrepreneur. Business was booming. I turned away more clients than I accepted because I was still really busy with my college classes. I wanted to expand my personal training business by hiring other trainers and possibly opening my own gym, so after completing two years of college I asked my parents what they thought of my idea.

They were less than supportive. My mother discouraged me, and my grandparents and other older relatives warned me that if I took time off I would never return to complete my academic education. Taking their advice to heart I stayed in school until I earned my degree.

But to this day I wonder what would have happened if I had followed my passion and grown that two-person business into a bigger and more profitable enterprise. In hindsight I don't fault those who offered me advice. They were sincerely looking out for my best interests, and I certainly appreciated that.

Based on my experience, however, my advice to others is to follow your dreams and passions—even if that means striking out on your own and ignoring the advice of others—to take advantage of a golden opportunity that might come around only once in a lifetime.

WHAT NOT TO DO:
❐ Follow traditional advice

ADVICE:
❐ When you have a passion in life, explore it
   and see if you can make a living doing it.
❐ When parents and family give advice, they
   can only regurgitate what they have learned.
❐ Sometimes it's better not to listen to your advice
   pool and take the road less traveled.

MISSED OP:
A Mother's Regret

This morning, my car wouldn't start. Rather than go inside, wade through the piles of clothes, old magazines, dirty cups and dishes, and try to wake either of my two adult children and ask for a ride, I walked half a mile down the road and caught the bus.

It was a nice morning. I wore my ballet flats, so the walk was pleasant. As I walked, I concentrated on the sound my shoes made over the gravel, I thought about the different birds I heard and what types of birds they might be, I counted the number of white cars that drove by, I did whatever I could to keep myself from thinking about my house and the two children in it.

But when I arrived at the bus stop, there was a woman there with a young girl I assumed to be her daughter. She looked to be about six. She looked, in fact, a lot like my own daughter had at that age, with enviable thick, wavy, brown hair. The girl was holding her mother's hand and talking.

"If I find a lot of books on horses, will you help me carry them back?"

The mother smiled and patted the backpack that sat on the bench next to them. "That's why I brought this. But you're in charge of finding all the books, okay?" She caught me looking and smiled. "She's got her first project due in a week," she said.

"I want to be a vet," the girl said solemnly.

I smiled. "I remember when my own kids had school projects to do. It seems like quite a long time ago, now."

The mother patted her daughter's head. "The time really does go by so fast."

And then the bus pulled up, wheezing to a stop, the tires kicking up a cloud of dust. We climbed aboard and I chose a seat near the mother and daughter, close enough that I could continue to watch them, to hear their conversation.

The truth was, while I had a vague recollection of John having a science project due, or Casey having a book report to write up, I had no memories of being there to help them. This was not due to a failing memory but because my helping them with schoolwork had never happened. Sure, I got up with them in the morning and saw them off to school, but once classes were done, they spent their afternoons in the after-school program, or, as they got older, doing as they pleased.

Their father and I divorced when they were young, young enough that they barely remembered him. Although I fully believe in the merits of a two-parent household, his not being a part of their lives was a blessing in disguise. He drank too much and worked too little, and when he announced he was moving across the country, I said a silent prayer of thanks.

I got a job as the teller at our local bank. I put in long hours; I never said no to overtime, covering shifts, or doing the work that no one else wanted to do. I plastered a smile on my face even when I felt like screaming, I was meticulous in keeping track of every cent that touched my hands, and I made certain that not a single customer walked away from my window feeling anything less than satisfied.

It takes a lot out of a person being "on" all the time, and once my shift was over and requisite errands completed, I was eager to get home and go to bed. I'd slap together tuna sandwiches for supper, or mix up a box of Hamburger Helper. I worked whatever Saturday shift I could, and on Sundays, I slept in and then dedicated myself to the mountain of laundry that had accumulated during the week. On Sundays, the children had to fend for themselves.

"But can't we go to the playground today? They're having a model airplane demonstration." A query of this sort would come each week, from either John or Casey, sometimes both, and if it wasn't a model airplane demonstration, it was a visit to the library, the museum, a nature walk through the park.

"I'm sorry, guys," I'd said, each and every time.

As my position at the bank got higher, my paychecks got larger. I bought a house with the master bedroom downstairs, which meant John and Casey had free reign of the upstairs: two bedrooms, a full bathroom, and a family room, which I let them convert into the "chill space" furnished with a leather L-shaped couch, a big-screen TV, and all the latest technology accessories to go along with it. There was a constant stream of children coming and going from my house; word got out that John and Casey had the "cool mom" who let them do whatever they wanted and always kept the cupboards stocked with the best snacks.

Such rumors shouldn't have made me proud, but they did. My own childhood was one of hand-me-downs that never quite fit right and rummaging through the thrift store in the church basement. My parents were strict, demanding I complete all homework assignments before I was allowed to do anything else, insisting that they be able to call any friend's house I planned to go over to and speak to the appropriate parental authority. I never had many friends over.

So for a while, I was secretly thrilled. Sure, I worked long hours and was never home, but I knew John and Casey were enjoying themselves, doing what they wanted, having the sort of upbringing I never had. Their grades were okay, though John struggled in English. I hired a tutor so he'd be able to graduate with the rest of his class.

"Can't you tutor me, Ma?" he'd asked. "You're good in English."

I was good in English, and for half a second, I considered it. But then I shook my head. When on earth would I be able to fit that in? "Give Mrs. Rollins a chance. She's a retired schoolteacher. She knows exactly the sort of thing that's going to be on your English tests. She'll be able to help you. And if you don't like her, if you feel like you aren't learning anything, you don't have to keep seeing her, okay?"

He scowled. "You make it sound like she's my girlfriend."

He met with Mrs. Rollins enough times that he was able to pass English, though just barely. His grades certainly weren't high enough to get into a good college, but I assumed he'd enroll at the local community college, figure out what he wanted to do, eventually transfer to a four-year university.

"Yeah, sure, Ma," he'd said when I brought it up a few days after graduation. He'd come home after being out all night, eyes bleary, hair unkempt, clothes rumpled. "I gotta get some sleep."

He slept, and then he slept some more. During my lunch break, I'd circle jobs in the classifieds section and leave it each morning on the kitchen table for either John or Casey to look at. And there were jobs, good summer jobs that would've enabled either to earn some decent pocket money: ice cream scooper, landscaper, junior camp counselor. But every evening when I returned, the paper would be there in the exact same place, untouched. The sink would be overflowing with dishes, empty soda cans littered the counters, clothes strewn everywhere. You'd think I hadn't provided each of them with their own solid walnut bureau, or that neither of their rooms came equipped with a generous-sized walk-in closet.

It had been nearly nine years since John walked across the stage to receive his diploma; Casey would turn twenty-four next week. I still perused the classifieds on my lunch break, still left it on the kitchen table every morning, but it was out of habit now, not hope of either of them ever finding their paths. They followed their schedules as strictly as I followed my own work-dictated one: sleep late, eventually wandering into the kitchen to generate more dirty dishes. At some point, Casey would leave and go to her boyfriend's house, John would probably return back to his room and play video games or use his computer.

The bus lurched to a stop in front of the library. I watched the mother and daughter get off, holding hands. I couldn't help but wonder how different my children's lives might've turned out if I had taken them by their hands, led them to the library. To the park. To the museum. To any of the number of places that might have generated some interest, motivation or direction in their lives.

I resisted the urge to run after the mother and daughter, to try to get back every lost opportunity I'd had with my own children by living vicariously through two people I didn't even know.

WHAT NOT TO DO:
❏ Passively hope your children will set their goals on their own.

ADVICE:
❏ Show children how to create a plan that will get them to their long-term goals.
❏ Check on children to see if they are working and understanding the process of achieving their set goals.

MISSED OP:
Stock Market Strategy

Warren Buffet invests in part based on the theory of observing the masses and doing the opposite. When everyone is buying stocks it's usually when there is unwarranted euphoria in the market. What does he do? He sells into the strength and takes profits.

In the winter of 2009, my brother and I were watching the stock market come down from historical highs. Since the fall of 2008, my brother had been following some analysts who believed strongly the markets were overbought and would tumble.

The Dow did come down from about 14,000 to around 6,600. Was this a buying opportunity? Or was the world going to end and the market going to zero? No one can time the market, just as no one can see the future. But what could an investor do?

Knowing that history has a tendency to repeat itself, we could have looked at the past and applied it to the future. This often seems easier said than done, and each generation has different circumstances even within similar situations. The world is very different from what it was the last time the market saw the stress of early 2009. But what would someone like Warren Buffett do? And, maybe just as important, why would I look at him and consider his action as advice for my own action?

Well, Warren Buffett is only one of the richest individuals in the United States. He is also one of the best historical investors of his era. So what was his opinion on whether to invest or not? He was a buyer so he bought.

He stuck with his tried-and-true principle of buying solid companies at discounted prices. I would guess that there was not a single stock in any market that wasn't at a discount price in March 2009.

What did my brother and I do? We questioned whether or not the market would continue to drop so we waited. Shortly thereafter, the market turned around and we watched it climb back to the 11,000 range, not buying anything the whole way up.

Granted, we aren't millionaires or billionaires, but the basic principles that Mr. Buffett follows apply to even us. At that time my brother was managing hundreds of thousands of dollars of my father's money, certainly enough to make a good profit on a solid investment.

Many, many good companies' stocks doubled and tripled or even quadrupled during that period! What took my father his entire life to save, could have been doubled in a matter of months.

Why didn't we just look at someone like Warren Buffett and apply those principles that made him and other investors successful? Why didn't we step back and do a cost benefit analysis? Why didn't we seek advice from someone else to get another perspective?

Why didn't we list the pros and cons of investing in time-tested companies? Why?

Those questions have led me down the path of regret. The regret of missing an opportunity that could have changed my family's lives forever. Now I have to work on moving past the mental pain and suffering that missed opportunity has caused.

WHAT NOT TO DO:

❐ Sit and wait for perfect circumstances to happen.

ADVICE:

❐ Research and take action if that is where your goals point to.

MISSED OP:
Buried Dreams

My name is Stefanie Stewart and I met my husband, Andy, when we were both freshmen in college. One of our mutual friends fixed us up on a blind date. We went to a bit of a dive called Don's Diner. It really was an awful place, but it was the college hangout in those days.

Andy was so easy to talk to that I soon forgot the dirty surroundings and the stained table tops. We ate our hamburgers and talked about everything and nothing. It seemed like time flew by on that first date. In fact, when it was over, neither of us seemed to want it to end. So we made plans to go on another date in a few days.

Over our four years in college, Andy and I had a lot of dates and each one seemed far too short. We never seemed to run out of things to talk about. Usually they were silly little things, like TV shows we liked or college assignments. Toward the end of senior year, however, our talks took a more serious turn.

I remember times when we would talk about our post-college plans. We were starting to panic about it a bit. It wasn't just because we weren't sure about our upcoming careers, but also because we lived on opposite sides of the country. When college was over, we might be over, too. Neither of us could stand the thought of that.

Andy had studied to be an advertising executive, but his heart wasn't really in it. I, on the other hand, wanted to be a teacher and it was my passion. So our directions, and the direction of our relationship, were unclear as we neared graduation.

Andy's family lived in Michigan and mine in Massachusetts. I wondered whether I should break it off with him entirely or try to maintain a long distance relationship after college. As it turned out, I didn't have to make that decision.

The week before graduation, Andy surprised me with an engagement ring. He begged me to marry him. I said yes, even though we were both basically feeling around in the dark, as far as post-college plans went.

I went back to Massachusetts for two years, getting a part-time teaching position. Andy, meanwhile, had gotten an advertising job in New York City, so we were closer than I'd planned, at least. We visited each other as often as we could and talked on the phone every day at least twice, but it was still hard.

After two years, Andy bought a house in New York and we were finally married, but I found it hard to adjust to life in the big city. Teaching jobs were tough to get and the pay was low. I was under constant stress to try to pull my own weight in the relationship.

During all of that, Andy and I sat down one day and had another of our famous talks. We had never discussed children before, but the subject came up. We both agreed that we wanted at least two kids, preferably a boy and a girl. Of course, we would have been happy with two boys or two girls, as long as they were healthy.

But we both also agreed that a small house in the middle of a bad neighborhood in New York City was no place to raise a family. So we decided to hold off and save our money to get a big house out in the country somewhere. We both wanted the "white picket fence" ideal that most people have.

It was soon after that discussion that Andy's mother became ill. We were forced to pull up stakes in New York and go to Michigan to help her recover. I didn't mind. After all, his family was now my family. Besides, we wouldn't have to pay rent there, so we could save money easier, or so I thought.

Andy's mother turned out to be sicker than we thought. She was chronically ill for about seven years before she finally passed away. It was another year after that before we could get all of her affairs settled before we could plan where to live next. We didn't really have to think about it because my parents offered to take us in until we found someplace new to stay. Of course, that meant moving back to Massachusetts.

I was thrilled to be back in my hometown, and I had no shortage of job offers from old friends, but none of them were in the teaching field. Nevertheless, I did what I had to get by. Andy, meanwhile, took the new move as an adventure. He decided to use some of his skills in a new way and applied for a job at a local newspaper office. He got the job, but the pay was low.

My mom and dad surprised us after we had been home a year, with our own little guest house that they had built in the backyard. It seemed like we were there to stay. I was thinking that we could finally start a family.

By then we were in our mid-thirties, and I was feeling my biological clock ticking away. Andy knew how I felt, but he was working long hours at the newspaper office and we seemed to be growing apart a bit. I didn't like how things were going, but I didn't want to put any more pressure on him than he already had.

The next few years passed by in a sort of dull routine until I finally turned forty. Andy asked me what I wanted for my birthday and I told him I really wanted to finally have kids. He was all for that, now that we finally had decent jobs and a roof over our heads. However, it didn't work out that way.

We tried to have kids on our own for what seemed like ages. Then we finally went for fertility treatments. The treatments didn't take, so we saw more specialists. The specialists told me what I basically already knew. I had missed my opportunity to have children.

Andy and I went home. I collapsed into bed crying hysterically. I told him that I felt awful because we had let life's circumstances get in the way of the lives that we wanted to have. We still loved each other, but I always felt like I buried the babies we never had along with dreams. And it isn't a feeling I would wish on any mother or potential mother.

WHAT NOT TO DO:

❐ Lose focus on your goals.

ADVICE:

❐ Discuss your goals with the important people in your life.
❐ Take action at some point; there will never be that perfect moment that so many wait for.

References

1 Castellan, Jr., N. John, ed. <u>Individual and Group Decision Making</u>. New Jersey: Lawrence Erlbaum Associates, 1993

2 Collins, W. Andrew; Maccoby, Eleanor E.; Steinberg, Laurence; Hetherington, E. Mavis; Bornstein, Marc H. "Contemporary research on parenting: The case for nature and nurture". <u>American Psychologist</u>.,Vol 55(2), 218-232. Feb 2000

3 U.S. Department of Health and Human Services, Administration for Children, National Center on Child Abuse and Neglect. <u>Third National Incidence Study of Child Abuse and Neglect (NIS-3)</u>. Washington, DC: 1996

4 Chapman, Daniel Ethan, ed. <u>Examining Social Theory</u>. New York: Peter Lang Publishing, 2010

5 McCormack, Mark H. <u>What They Don't Teach You in the Harvard Business School</u>. Book Views Inc., New York 1984

6 Duke University Medical Center. "Aerobic Exercise Improves Cognitive Functioning Of Men And Women". <u>Science Daily</u>. 17 Jan. 2001. Web. 2 Oct. 2011.

7 Goldman, W.P.. "Absence of cognitive impairment or decline in preclinical Alzheimer's disease." <u>Neurology</u> 56:361-367 February 13, 2001

8 Deci, Edward., Ryan, Richard, "Hedonia, eudaimonia, and well-being: an introduction". <u>Journal of Happiness Studies</u>. Springer Netherlands, 1389-4978, 2008

9 Burgess P.W., Veitch E., De Lacy Costello A., Shallice T. The cognitive

and neuroanatomical correlates of multitasking. <u>Neuropsychologia</u>, 38 (6), pp. 848-863. 20. 2000

10 Citrin, Jim, "Leadership by Example". <u>Yahoo Finance</u>, January 30, 2007. http://finance.yahoo.com/expert/article/leadership/23188

11 Howe, Michael J. A., Davidson, Jane W., Sloboda, John A.. <u>Innate talents: Reality or myth?</u> Behavioral and Brain Sciences 21 (3):399-407. 1998

12 Bridgeland, John M., DiIulio, John J., Jr., Morison, Karen Burke. "The Silent Epidemic: Perspectives of High School Dropouts". <u>A report by Civic Enterprises in association with Peter D. Hart Research Associates for the Bill & Melinda Gates Foundation</u>. iii. March 2006, http://www.gatesfoundation.org/united-states/Documents/TheSilentEpidemic3-06Final.pdf

13 Whitaker, Bill. "High School Dropouts Costly for American Economy". <u>CBS Evening News</u>. May 28, 2010. http://www.cbsnews.com/stories/2010/05/28/eveningnews/main6528227.shtml

14 Murphy, Joseph. <u>The Power of Your Subconscious Mind</u>. New York: Penguin, 2008.

15 About USM Team. "Undecided is Not a Major". <u>Fast Web</u>. September 02, 2009. http://www.fastweb.com/college-search/articles/1529-undecided-is-not-a-major

16 Duffett, Ann. Johnson, Jean. "Life After School ". <u>Public Agenda</u>. 1-50. 2005. http://www.publicagenda.org/files/pdf/life_after_high_school.pdf

17 Centers for Disease Control and Prevention. National Vital Statistics Reports, Volume 58, Number 25 – Births, Marriages, Divorces, and Deaths. <u>Provisional Data</u>. 2009.

Index

About the Authors

Keith Nelson learned what not to do when presented with many opportunities. As a result, he gained a wealth of diverse experience and a keen insight on how to reverse engineer a failed outcome into a process for success. Nelson completed his educational background with majors in Criminal Justice, Liberal Arts, a bachelor's degree in Exercise Physiology, and a master's degree in Education and is currently working toward his Ph.D in Health Psychology. His enthusiasm to explore new opportunities led him through an interesting assortment of careers, including an insurance claims representative, small-business owner and entrepreneur, website designer, personal trainer, natural bodybuilder, Special Agent with the Drug Enforcement Administration, teacher, coach and author. Through this assorted background he has gained the experience necessary to make him an expert in the area of recognizing and dissecting various opportunities.

Anthony Rienzi began creating opportunities for himself at an early age. During high school he and his brothers started a small business that flourished into a thriving, expanding enterprise. After earning a degree in accounting, he worked for several years as an executive sales representative and was involved in various aspects of business management. Circumstances and choices led to a career in law enforcement, and he served as police officer for the NYPD. Later he became a Special Agent with the Drug Enforcement Administration and ultimately achieved a position as a Special Agent within the Federal Bureau of Investigation. His insatiable desire to achieve more and share his knowledge led to the writing of this book, which will enable others to benefit from his diverse experience.

As DEA and FBI Special Agents, the authors received training to use fact-based interviewing techniques and investigative analyzing skills. They applied these same skills to break down missed opportunities to identify what went wrong and how it could have been corrected. Through analyzing their personal experiences and interviewing other people, the authors determined common facts of failure and created an outline of skills and techniques for success, which is presented in this straightforward informational book

Nelson and Rienzi believe that their knowledge gained through multiple missed opportunities can guide others through their decision-making processes so that they can seize life-changing opportunities. The authors are eager to share their experiences and are excited for readers to gain invaluable benefits that will help them improve their lives, reach their goals, and live out their dreams.

JUL '12

RIVERHEAD FREE LIBRARY
330 COURT STREET
RIVERHEAD, NY 11901

CPSIA information can be obtained at www.ICGtesting.com
Printed in the USA
BVOW040050050612

291721BV00002B/1/P